DEDICATED TO MY MOM & DAD
(They know who they are)

Rock n' Blues Harmonica

A Beginner's Guide to Jamming

By
Jon Gindick

With illustrations by
Mark Zingarelli

Calligraphy by
Holly Fox

Cover illustration by
Art & Kim Ellis

Cross Harp Press
Visalia — Los Angeles

Introduction

The lights are low as you step to the microphone. In the audience you see faces, the faces of people who have come to hear the hottest band in town—with *you* playing the harmonica.

The lights brighten and dim. This means it's time to start. "One-two-three-four!" shouts the drummer. His sticks bang on the drumheads in a frenzy of rhythym. The guitarist strums his opening chord and the bass player dances across the stage, the *boom, boom, boom* of his instrument providing a low-toned support.

The music has started; a churning brew of rhythm and sound that moves people to their feet and out to the dance floor. Now it's your turn. You place your harmonica to your puckered lips. You blow, you draw, you warble and wail. Notes shoot through space, tumbling one after the other, curving and burning through the music.

The audience breaks into applause. This is the sound they've come to hear; the sound of your harmonica accompanying electric guitar, drums and bass. It's the sound of emotion and skill, creativity and fun. It's the sound of today's music. And man, there's nothing else like it.

Rock n' Blues Harmonica is about this sound and the experience of creating it. The book works like this. In Chapter I, you'll read how Adam and Eve discovered notes, scales, chords and chord progressions in the Garden of Eden. While you don't need to memorize this information to play harmonica, getting the basic idea will give you a strong sense of how music is organized. And *this* will help you make music on any instrument, both solo and with a band.

Harmonica instruction begins with Chapter II. You'll meet the world's first rock and blues band, the Cave Boys, and take lessons from their harmonica player, Stone. With Stone's help, you'll learn what kind of harmonica to buy, how to make your first sounds, how to play chords, chord progressions, single notes, blues riffs, how to play with a band, how to play solo, how to bend notes, how to play melodies, how to play in three different harp styles (Cross Harp, Straight Harp and Slant Harp), how to improvise and much more.

Mostly, this book is about jamming; loosening up and letting go; melting into the harp as you play the music that pours out of your soul. It's about feeling a rhythm, discovering a melody and turning it into a jam session. In short, it's about having fun with music, and maybe getting good. Real good.

So pull out your harmonica (Chapter II tells you what kind) and start making some passionate noises. You've got the music in you. Let *Rock n' Blues Harmonica* help bring it out.

Table of Contents

ONE

The Night Music was Discovered

(Theory for Beginners)

It was a magical night. The stars were twinkling and everything was new – including music. This was the night Adam and Eve discovered the note, the chord, and the chord progression. It was the night music was born.

Eight Little Sounds

As everyone knows, music was discovered by Adam and Eve in the Garden of Eden.

Here's how it happened.

One morning Adam was thirsty. He'd been running around the Garden discovering things and giving them names. Cottonmouth (which he'd not yet named) was driving him crazy. So he asked Eve to bring him a glass of iced tea.

Now Eve was a flaxen haired beauty with great legs and a terrific sense of humor. She was also very intelligent. She filled a glass with tea and ice and handed it to Adam. As he took it from her hand, the spoon accidentally struck the glass.

What happened next was incredible. It was a *noise*, a high-pitched ringing tone. Eve's sensitive eardrums could feel this noise vibrating.

"What's that?" Eve asked.

Adam, of course, knew everything. And what he didn't know, he made up. Still, he had no idea what that sound was.

"A..." he began.

"A what?" demanded Eve.

"A...a...it's an **A**," he said, and drank a little more of the tasty tea. As if by miracle, the spoon struck the glass once again.

The glass, being emptier by one swallow, made a tone that was one swallow higher.

"And what's that?" Eve asked.

"Do I have to tell you everything?" snapped Adam. "It's a **B**!" He gave Eve a smarter-than-thou look and sipped again from the glass.

"Typical male," Eve said. But the lady was getting curious. She tapped on the glass with the spoon. Being a little emptier than before, the resulting tone was a little higher.

"And I suppose that's a **C**," Eve said.

"You got it," muttered Adam. He took another swallow. "Tingggg!" sang the glass as Eve struck it with the spoon.

"For crimany sakes, woman," Adam growled. But they both knew that what had occurred was a **D**.

And so it went. Adam drank. Eve played an **E**. Adam sipped once more. Eve clanged a one-beat boogie on an **F**. Again Adam sipped. The new tone was dubbed **G**.

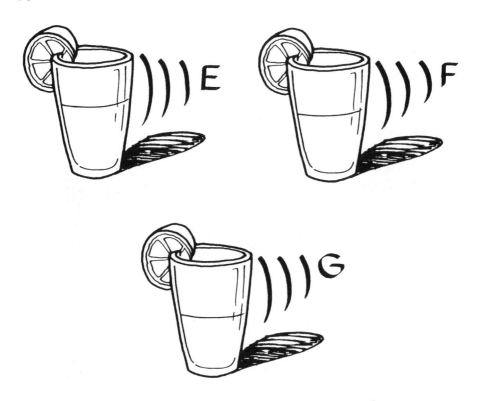

"Big deal," Adam said. He took another swallow. He had now drunk half the iced tea that was originally in the glass. Eve struck the glass with the spoon.

A sound occurred.

"Boy, that sounds familiar," said Eve.

"Of course,"Adam said. "It's the same note we played in the beginning." The highly caffeinated iced tea was beginning to have an effect on him.

"It's an **A**, but a higher **A** than we played when the glass was full. What we've done is play a ladder of sounds starting from **A**." And in his rich tenor voice Adam started to sing:

"**A B C D E F G A!**"

"You see, Eve, when the glass was full, and the spoon hit it, vibrations came out of the glass into the air. You may not believe this, but I counted 440 vibrations per second. That was the **A** sound.

"Now, I drank a little bit more and you banged the glass again. Since the glass was a bit emptier, the vibration into the air (and our eardrums) was faster. In fact, it was right around 510 vibrations per second. That's the sound we called a **B**."

"I get it," Eve said. "Each time you made the glass a little emptier, the vibrations it made were a little faster, and the resulting tone was higher. But why is the high **A** the same as the low **A**?"

"Don't you see?" Adam said. "The glass vibrated twice as fast, and that makes the sound twice as high."

"I suppose you think that makes you twice as smart," Eve said with a giggle.

"Of course," laughed Adam. "Now let's assign some names to all this. We'll call each sound a NOTE. That gives us an **A** note, a **B** note, a **C** note, and so forth.

"And each ladder of sounds that goes from **A** to **A**, or from **B** to **B** is a SCALE. If you start on an **A**, you have an **A** scale. If you start on a **C**, it's a **C** scale. Not bad, eh?"

"How come you have to name everything?" Eve asked. "Some strange psychological compulsion?"

"And the distance between a high **A** and the low **A**...we'll call that an OCTAVE."

"Call it what you want," Eve said. "Just answer me this. What's it good for?"

"Get me eight glasses of iced tea and we'll find out," Adam said.

Sweet Harmony

That evening, strange sounds were heard in the Garden. There was laughter. Then came a new way of talking that rose and fell in the craziest ways. And then, even weirder, came a succession of high-pitched, ringing sounds. *Bong! Clang! Boing!*

It was Adam and Eve, sitting in the glow of the fire, pleasantly blasted on bongo juice, surrounded by glasses, each filled with a different amount of iced tea. Adam was beating his hands on his haunches and snapping his fingers, giving Eve a rhythm in which to explore the tones of the glasses.

"Yeah, yeah," Adam sang. "Yeah, yeah."

"Hey!" cried Eve. "Listen to this!" She was holding a spoon in each hand. "If I strike a **C** note at the same time that I strike an **E**, dig it: the sounds combine."

Firelight flickering on her face, Eve clanged the spoons on the glass filled to **C** and on the glass filled to **E** at the same time.

The two tones collaborated and faded into the night.

"That was beautiful," Adam said. "Do it again."

Once again, Eve struck the **C** and **E** glasses at the same time. The vibrations intertwined to form something rich and sweet.

"What *was* that?" asked a delighted Eve.

"Think I'll call that a...a...a HARMONY," said Adam. "Yes, a harmony is when two notes played at the same time blend together to form a new, combined sound."

"Fair enough," said Eve. "But what happens if I strike the **C** and **D** glasses at the same time?"

To answer her own question, Eve banged her spoons on the two glasses.

Although the **C** and **D** did not clash, neither did they form the beautiful blend that came from the **C** and **E**. Eve frowned. What was going on here?

"I get it!" she suddenly cried. "The **C** and **E** notes are the first and third notes of the **C** scale. **C** is number 1, **D** is number 2, **E** is number 3, and so on.

"If you want a nice blending harmony using the **C**, you strike the 1st and 3rd notes of the **C** scale at the same time.

"And if you want this blend to use the **G** sound, you strike the 1st and 3rd notes of the **G** scale."

To prove her point, Eve struck her spoons on the **G** and **B** glasses. The two sounds combined beautifully.

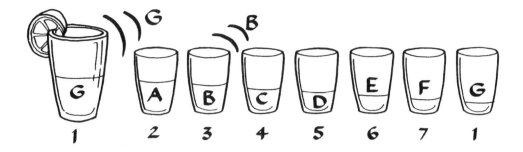

"See?" cried Eve. "If I play the 1st and 3rd notes of this simple scale at the same time, they merge together. I've got an idea. Let's call the 1st and 3rd notes HARMONIZING NOTES!"

Suddenly, Eve realized her mistake. It was Adam's job to name things. She could discover, but *he* had to name. She looked at him nervously. Would he be angry?

Adam only smiled. Eve looked beautiful with firelight rippling across her long, flowing hair. "Yeah," Adam said, a crazy grin on his face. "The 1st and 3rd notes come together and harmonize when played at the same time. Just like us, baby."

The Incredible Chord

And so the night went. Much bongo juice was consumed. The laughing, the strange way of talking, the piercing sounds of glasses struck with spoons...it was all so new. Even The Landlord stopped to cock His head and listen.

Meanwhile, the couple in the Garden were making important discoveries about this thing called music. They learned that not only did the 1st and 3rd notes of each scale come together and harmonize when played at the same time – but that the 5th note of the scale also harmonized.

Adam called this combination of three harmonizing notes played at the same time a CHORD. To play a **C** chord, Eve would strike the glasses that produced a **C** note and an **E** note, the 1st and 3rd notes of the **C** scale. At exactly the same time, Adam would bang on the 5th note of the scale – the **G** note.

The **C, E,** and **G** notes flowed into each other and produced what Adam called a **C** chord.

Then, Eve struck the 1st, 3rd and 5th notes of the **G** scale. **G** was the 1st note, **B** was the 3rd note and **D** was the 5th note. This produced the **G** chord.

20

another major chord

G 1   B 3   D 5

"Hey!" shouted Adam. I think we're on to something!"

Without thinking what he was doing, he picked up the 6th glass of the **C** scale and started to drink. He had half a swallow in his mouth when Eve squealed, "What are you doing?"

Coughing, half-choking, face red with embarrassment, Adam put the glass back in its number 6 spot. "I thought it was bongo juice," he started to say, but stopped himself.

"I know *exactly* what I'm doing," he said imperiously.

"And what *exactly* is that?" demanded Eve.

"I wanted to see what would happen if I made the 6th note a little higher by making the glass half a swallow emptier. Know what I mean? Now the glass is halfway between the 6th and 7th note of the **C** scale. It's a 6½ glass."

"Real sharp, flathead!" shouted Eve.

But Adam knew the best discoveries often occurred by mistake. "Let's see what happens when you play the 1st, 3rd and 5th notes of **C** scale at the same time that I bang on the 6½ note."

"Whatever you say," answered Eve. She banged her spoons on the 1st, 3rd and 5th glasses while Adam played his 6½ glass.

the bluesy 7th chord

C   E   G   B FLAT*

1   3   5   6½

What a sound! It was odd, yet powerful, speaking of the ironies of a life filled with passions and disappointments, new loves and sad goodbyes. All this was pretty heady stuff for Adam who had spent all his young life in the Garden of Eden. Still, he must have had a sense of what was to come.

"This chord, this combination of 1st, 3rd, 5th and 6½ notes of a scale shall henceforth be called a 7th CHORD (in this case C7th)."

He looked triumphantly at Eve and wobbled a little. "And the 7th chord shall be the mainstay, the distinguishing characteristic of the type of music that will someday be called THE BLUES."

At that, Eve grabbed Adam and laughingly pulled him to the ground, covering him with kisses. "I'll give you the blues," she murmered, pulling him closer.

---

* The term **B** flat refers to the note halfway between the **A** and the **B**. This note could also be called **A** sharp, but rarely is. Including sharps and flats (also known as halfsteps), there are 12 notes in a scale: **A** flat, **A, B** flat, **B, C, C** sharp, **D, E** flat, **E, F, F**sharp, **G**.

Majors and Minors

Well, they played and played. All of it in the key of **C**, of course.

KEY? That's the word Adam used to identify the idea that in music, if you start a song on a **C** note, you usually end the song on a **C** note. Thus you're playing in the key of **C**.

In the same vein, when you start a song on an **E** note, you usually end the song on the **E** note – and are playing in the key of **E**.

At any rate, as Adam and Eve arranged and rearranged glasses and struck them with spoons, they learned a few things about music that would intrigue musicians for years to come.

1. Woman likes to boogie as much as man.

2. Clinking spoons on glasses of iced tea is a hell of a way to make music.

3. When playing in the key of **C**, you can play the basic chord, the major chord, by striking the 1st, 3rd and 5th glasses of the scale.

4. You can get a blues sound by including the 6½ note with the 1st, 3rd and 5th.

5. You can get a mysterious, eerie sounding chord by playing the 1st, 2½ and 5th glasses of a scale. Adam called this a MINOR CHORD.

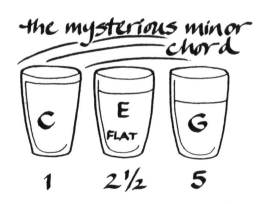

the mysterious minor chord

C   E FLAT   G

1   2½   5

6. And, playing the 1st, 3rd, 5th and 6th produces a jazzy sounding chord. This was called a MAJOR 6th.

In fact, the list of chords Adam and Eve discovered that evening was endless. There were no limits on the tones these notes could combine to form.

As Eve went from one chord to the next, it was easy to imagine her the precursor of today's electric guitarist. She shook her head and her long hair swished back over her shoulder. She lifted her spoon-holding hands and brought them down in a wide arc, almost as though she were strumming the glasses.

"Yeah, yeah," Adam sang. Although he didn't know it, his girlfriend Eve was on the verge of a new discovery – a discovery that would create the chord framework for the types of music that would one day be known as country western, blues, punk, disco, reggae, folk, rock a' billy, gospel, tex-mex, schlock and rock and roll.

This discovery was the I-IV-V CHORD PROGRESSION. Here's how it happened.

The I-IV-V of Music

Eve arranged the iced-tea glasses into rows of major chords.

First, she bonged the **C** chord 4 times in a row. Then she clanged on the **F** chord, the chord 4 glasses up the scale from the **C**.

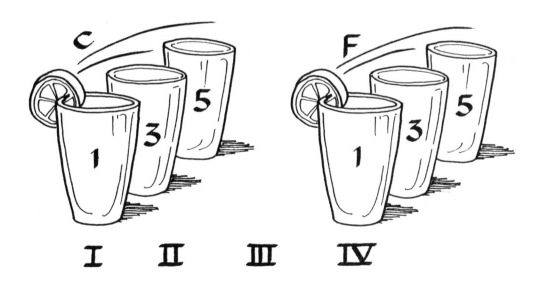

She played these two chords over and over and it sounded terrific. Four beats on the I chord, four beats on the IV chord. This was the birth of the TWO-CHORD JAM.

But there was much more to learn. This was when Eve discovered she could add to the two-chord feeling by bonging the **G** chord, the chord 5 glasses up the scale from the **C** chord.

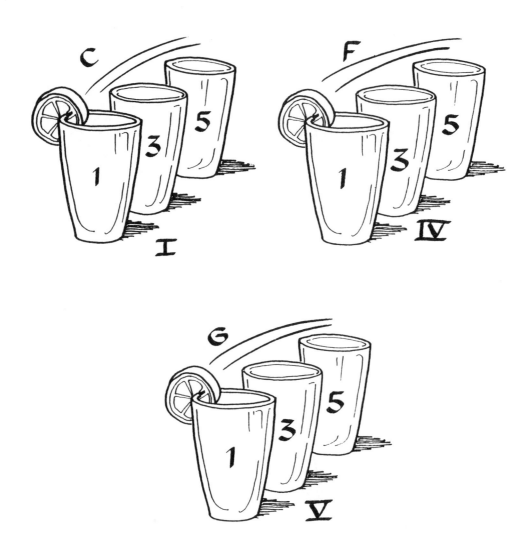

This V chord (the **G** chord when played in the key of **C**) took the music further away from the I chord. It added a sense of transition, a feeling of drama and *tension*.

It sounded great to pound out a beat on the I chord, then the IV chord, then back to the I chord. Now was the time to play the V chord, slip down to the IV chord, and with an air of finality and resolution, return to the I chord.

Wow! This I-IV-V progression really made sense. It put the sounds into a cycle, gave them a beginning and an end. It created and resolved tension. It organized sound to tell a story.

Even Adam was amazed as Eve hunched over her rows of iced tea glasses and played these beautiful sequences of harmonizing notes. He *had* to jam. But how? How does one musician accompany another? Spoon in hand, the original man set out to make a new discovery.

Accompanying the I-IV-V Chord Progression

Adam knew Eve was playing her I-IV-V chord progression in the key of **C**. Following a hunch, he started banging on his **C** glass. It sounded pretty good! While Eve went from one chord to the next, all Adam had to do was play the 1st note of the scale.

But Eve, swinging spoons like a maestro, wanted more. "C'mon!" she shouted over the loud clinking of iced tea glasses. "Get it on!"

So get it on is exactly what Adam did. But he paid attention,too. Soon he realized that certain iced tea glasses sounded great no matter where the music was in the I-IV-V progression.

The glasses that always sounded so great were none other than the 1st, 3rd and 5th notes of the **C** scale. These were the harmonizing notes that made up the **C** chord.

By accenting these harmonizing notes (playing them longer and playing them louder), and using other notes in the **C** scale as stepping stones between one harmonizing note and another, Adam created melodic patterns that swirled confidently through Eve's I-IV-V progression of chords.

Amazingly, it didn't matter when Adam hit the 1st, 3rd or 5th note. Each would work at any point in the chord progression.

Now Adam decided to get fancy. He started banging on the 2½ glass, the glass which was left over from the minor chord. What a sound! Sexy, sultry, bluesy. He banged the 2½ glass again, and *again*. Like the 1st, 3rd and 5th notes, it worked through all of Eve's chord changes.

But this 2½ note did more than simply accompany the I-IV-V chord progression. Somehow, it changed the music, made it hard. Made it tense. Made it bluesy.

It was a BLUES HARMONIZING NOTE.

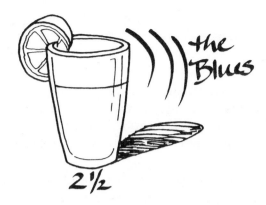

2½

"Alright!" shouted Eve. As the original blues lady bonged a steady beat on the I-IV-V progression, Adam explored every nook and cranny of the **C** scale. He banged the 1st note six or seven times (it didn't matter). Then he clanged the 5th note, the 4th note, the 2½ note, and finally returned to the 1st note.

Then he was off again, at one time or another striking a spoon on every glass he could see. Some glasses sounded terrible, and some sounded like they were born to make music. Finally, through trial and error, Adam discovered the BLUES SCALE.

Starting with the **C** note and going up the scale, the blues scale went: 1   2½   4   5   6½   1. *

What a sound this blues scale created! What a feeling! Eve, by now, was playing progressive jazz chords, using minors, major sixths, altering the chord progression in innumerable ways, playing rock, reggae, blues and country western, yet never leaving the key of **C**. Adam, too, was swept away by the ringing tones of iced tea glasses. Eve could play any chord she wanted, and as long as she always returned to her **C** chord, her I chord, Adam's wonderful new blues scale would not make a mistake.

This was the kind of music that could go on forever. (And in a way, it has.) But even the original man and woman occasionally got tired.

As the sun rose in the eastern sky and the light of a new day shone on the young, musical world, Adam yawned. Eve yawned. The tight rhythms of Eve's chord progression and Adam's accompaniment took slack. Mistakes were made, but neither musician cared.

Finally, the music stopped altogether. The Landlord took a deep breath as Adam and Eve crawled into the trees and fell asleep in each others arms.

~~~

Adam and Eve awakened with hangovers the following afternoon. A few days later they were asked to leave the Garden for good. It seems Adam had hooked up iced tea glasses to amplifiers and had been playing them at outrageous volumes.

On her way out of the Garden into the Wilderness, Eve picked a piece of bark off a tree, a tree Adam had previously named the boo boo tree. She chewed on the sweet bark as she walked. Then, before she knew it, she was holding the reed-like thing between her teeth and blowing and drawing.

What a strange sounds that piece of vibrating bark made! It was almost like a duck. *Wa Wo Wa!*

Adam turned to Eve. "What's that?" he asked. "What are those sounds?"

Eve only smiled.

Notes

* The NOTE is the basic unit of music.

* Notes form SCALES. If the first note of the scale is a **C**, this is a **C** scale. If the first note is a **G**, it's a **G** scale.

* When played at the same time, the 1st, 3rd and 5th notes of a scale HARMONIZE to form a MAJOR CHORD. The 1st, 3rd and 5th notes of a **C** scale play a **C** major chord. Likewise for an **A** or a **B** scale.

* The structure of most rock, blues and country western music is built around the I-IV-V CHORD PROGRESSION.

* Moving from one chord to the next forms a CYCLE. The I chord is the HOME BASE, the place where the music usually starts and ends. The IV chord moves the music further away from home base. The V chord moves it further still. Being away from home creates MUSICAL TENSION. Returning home RESOLVES THE TENSION.

* There are many VARIATIONS to the above cycle, but the I-IV-V progression is the foundation on which they're based.

* A simple way to ACCOMPANY another instrument playing the I-IV-V chord progression (or a variation) is to play musical patterns that emphasize the 1st, 3rd and 5th notes of the I chord's scale. No matter what chord the music plays, these HARMONIZING NOTES will not make a mistake.

* This accompaniment can sound BLUESY by including the 2½ note of the I chord's major scale.

* If this leaves you slightly confused, don't worry. Many harmonica players know much less than you about the structure of music and play just great!

TWO

First Sounds of the Harmonica

Now that you have an idea how music is organized, it's time to pull out your harmonica and start making your own sounds. In Chapter II, you'll meet the world's first rock band, The Cave Boys, their harp player, Stone, and you will learn the harmonica essentials – what kind of harp to play, how to make your first sounds, and how to play chords and single notes.

Legend of the Cave Boys

From what little we know, the world's first rock band was a four person group called the Cave Boys. They played drums, bass, guitar and harmonica – amplifying their instruments through valuable electric tree stumps for which they had scoured the countryside.

The legend also tells us of Umm, the beautiful female vocalist who joined the Cave Boys and led them to stardom with such prehistoric hits as "Tango in the Tarpits" and "Funky Dinosaur."

The story that hasn't yet been told is that of Stone, the band's harmonica player. He started as a boy on a hillside with only the crickets and the coyotes for accompaniment. He went on to make the sweetest blues and rock harmonica sounds the world has ever heard.

What were Stone's secrets? How was he able to make that harmonica bend and warble with so much feeling – and always in perfect accompaniment to the band's pounding I-IV-V chord progression? How was he able to play bluesy sounding Cross Harp, then melodic Straight Harp, and finally exotic, minor key Slant Harp? Was he a human being or some bizarre musical god?

This story now belongs to you. All you need is a harmonica, a pair of lips, and a sense of fun. Dig it. Stone didn't know a lot about music, but he knew how to play it. As you're about to discover, you can play it too.

What Model of Harmonica?

To play blues, rock, folk or country western harp, you need a 10 HOLED DIATONIC HARMONICA. (see picture on following page) If this is your first harmonica, key of C is recommend. Here's a few good ones:

Marine Band—Here's most popular harmonica in the world; it's basic design created in 1896. True, the wooden mouthpiece is harder to play. The wood swells, is harder to slide—yet the ol' Marine Band provides the warmest tone and is the favorite of those serious, tough-lipped Chicago blues players.

Golden Melody—a professional instrument that emphasises technical clarity and precise tuning. Some feel it lacks the warmth of the other harps, and yet offers the advantage of "equal tuning" and extreme ease of playing and bending. It is also the easiest harp for "overblows" (see page 206).

Lee Oskar—Designed and manufactured by one of our greatest players, Lee Oskar, the' Oskie seems to give an easier shot at the single note. It offers exchangable reed plates so when a harmonica wears out, you can replace the reeds instead of having to buy a new harp.

Special 20—This wonderful little harmonica is shaped like the M.B., but uses a plastic comb instead of wood. Has a Marine Band feel without the disadvantages.. The result is an easily-cupped, sweet-toned, and easy-sliding harp.

Big River—Here's the latest technology in harps. At a lesser price, the River is the easiest-playing of all. Tone's not as rich and the shape a tad thicker then traditional, but it's excellent harmonica for starting and possibly staying with.

If this is your first harmonica, the key of C is recommended.

A Closer Look

Stone's harmonicas were carefully carved from the tusk of wild boar with reeds fashioned from the hard bark of the boo boo tree. There are only a few of these harps in existence today. Of course, they're priceless.

The rest of us play harmonicas with nickle plated covers, wood or plastic air chambers, and brass reeds.

From 1 through 10, each air chamber (or hole) is numbered. Inside each air chamber are two reeds: thin strips of metal of different lengths. The reed on the ceiling of the air chamber vibrates when air is BLOWN through the harmonica. The reed on the floor of the chamber responds when air is sucked or DRAWN through the harp.

Thus, each hole has a blow note and a draw note.

On holes 1 through 6, blow notes are lower than draw notes. The situation reverses itself on holes 7 through 10. Up here draw notes are lower than blow notes.

When this book refers to, say, 4 draw, it means suck on hole 4. Four blow, or *4 blow*, means to blow on hole 4. In the charts and graphs, the number 4 with a circle around it means 4 draw. An uncircled 4 means 4 blow.

Here are some additional facts about your harmonica:

* The key of your harp is etched on its right end. If you own a **C** harp, 1 blow plays a **C** note. On a **D** harp, 1 blow is a **D** note.

* When playing, the key of your harmonica and the numbers identifying each hole should be facing up.

* The only complete scale on your harmonica goes from 4 blow through 7 blow. Holes 1 through 4 and 7 through 10 have "missing notes."

Lay Out of Notes on C Harp

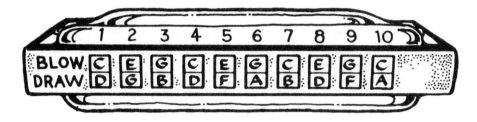

* Almost all the notes on your harp can be expressed in octaves. For instance, 1 draw is the same note as 4 draw and 8 draw. They are simply an octave apart. One blow is the same note as 4 blow and 7 blow. Three blow is the same note as 6 blow and 9 blow.

* From **G** (your lowest harp) through **F** sharp (your highest harmonica), the 12 different keyed harmonicas are organized exactly the same. If, by playing 6 blow, 5 draw, 4 draw, 4 blow, 3 draw, 3 blow, you can play a blues scale on your **G** harp, this same pattern of blows and draws will play a blues scale on your **F** sharp harmonica.

The only difference is that your **G** harp's blues scale will be very low in tone, and the blues scale on your **F** sharp harmonica will be quite high. This is the PRINCIPLE OF HARMONICA RELATIVITY: although they play in different keys, all harps have the same relationships of notes, scales and chords.

The Principle of Harmonica Relativity is both a convenience and a hassle. The hassle is that you need to carry around a number of different key harmonicas, and you never seem to have the one you need. The convenience is that you only have to learn a blues riff (pattern of notes) once to play it all different keys.

First Sounds

Even Stone had to start somewhere.

The first sounds he made on his harmonica were rough and uncontrolled. "Will you shut up?" his father would yell as the young harp player sat in the corner of the cave and practiced. "You're going to attract dinosaurs!"

Amazingly, no dinosaurs came. And, as Stone became more familiar with his harp – the feel of it in his mouth, the sensation of sounds produced by blowing and drawing, changing the sounds by changing the shape of his lips and mouth – his music became admired instead of scorned.

Now it's your turn. Numbers facing up, put your harmonica to your lips. Make your mouth big enough to cover holes 1, 2, 3 and 4 at the same time. You may want to stretch a finger across holes 5, 6, 7, 8, 9 and 10 so you know where holes 1, 2, 3 and 4 are.

Keeping your mouth relaxed, blow gently into holes 1, 2, 3 and 4. Excellent! You've just played a major chord, the combination of 1-3-5 harmonizing notes that were discovered by Adam and Eve.

To play another major chord, draw on holes 1, 2, 3, 4. Listen as you play. This draw chord is higher than the blow chord. By going back and forth between the draw chord and the blow chord, you can play a simple two chord harmonica jam.

After you've explored the blows and draws of holes 1, 2, 3 and 4, slide the harp up one hole so you're playing 2, 3, 4 and 5. Blow and draw and move the harp up another hole to 3, 4, 5 and 6. Blow and draw. Listen to the sounds of your harmonica. Make your breathing gentle and controlled as you slide the harp from one end to the other.

Some tips on moving the harmonica and playing chords:

1. Move the harp, not your head.

2. To make sure you're including hole number 1, place the low end of your harp in the corners of your lips.

3. If your chords have a bleating, forced quality, your mouth is too tight on the harp. Relax. Don't force the sounds. Clenching the harmonica between your teeth and blowing and drawing will give you an idea of how rich and full these chords can sound.

4. When blowing, let air escape over the top of your harp. This will improve your tone, keep you from running out of breath, and lighten the air pressure on the reeds.

With these suggestions in mind, continue exploring the sounds of your harmonica. Make your playing slow and lazy. Learn to relax when the harmonica is in your mouth.

Stomping

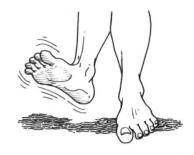

As you blow and draw your way up and down your harmonica, begin stomping a beat on the floor. Make this beat slow and steady. Count "1 – 2 – 1 – 2" or "1 – 2 – 3 – 4 – 1 – 2 – 3 – 4." Playing to a beat will give meaning and feeling to the sounds you make on your harp. Remember: rhythm is at least half of music.

You can also get a beat by listening to the mechanical hum of a washing machine, the clicking and slurping of windshield wipers, the dripping of a faucet, or the busy signal on a telephone. Metronomes, drum machines, drum records and even real live drummers have been known to work. The important thing is to play to a beat.

Tonguing

Make a long blow or draw sound on your harp. Now flick the tip of your tongue – as though you were saying *ta ta ta* – on the ridge behind your upper teeth.

This *ta ta ta* tonguing action will stop and start the air traveling through your harp. This will stop and start the sound of your harp. The result is total control of a crisp, rhythmic harp sound. Now you can play your blows and draws for four, eight, or sixteen beats each, and by tonguing quickly, make the harp sound as though you were playing fast enough to beat the devil.

But *fast* is not the only form of rhythm. Making some sounds long and others short as in *taaaaa ta* or *tata taaaaa taaaaaa* is also very effective.

Spend a few minutes using your tongue to put rhythm into your impromptu harp music. DO NOT stop your breath when you tongue. Keep the air flow moving and let your tongue play the percussion.

40

Train Jam

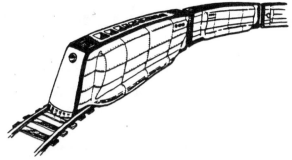

Although Stone never saw a train, he played train music like nobody's business. The harp sounds like a train when it huffs and puffs, builds up speed, goes faster and faster, and then, with the next station in view, slowly comes to a halt.

You can play train music (sometimes called Freight Harp) by going back and forth between the 1234 draw chord and the 1234 blow chord, giving each chord 1 beat. This is a I to IV chord jam.

(1234)	1234	(1234)	1234	(1234)
Draw	Blow	Draw	Blow	Draw
I	IV	I	IV	I

Start slowly, like a train leaving the station. Draw. Blow. Draw. Blow. Gradually go faster, letting air escape over the top of your harp on the blow chords.

Once your train is chugging down the track, you may want to try making a whistle sound. Draw holes 45 for eight beats, making these two notes cry out like the whistle of a train.

(45)
Waaaaaaaaaaaaaaaaaaaaaah!
V

Without hesitating, return to your 1234 draw and blow pattern, playing the draw chord *before* you blow. Now, begin slowing down, like a train that knows the station is only a mile away.

Slower still, Chugalug, chugalug, chugalug on your 1234 draw and 1234 blow.

And finally, bring your train into the station, home at last.

(45)
Waaaaaaaaaaaaaaaaaaaaaaaah!

The I-IV-V of Harmonica

Since the earliest times, the I-IV-V chord progression or blues cycle has served as the framework for popular music. Adam and Eve used it. Stone used it. Now it's your turn.

When playing the style of harmonica known as Cross Harp (see the next chapter), your I chord is played by drawing on holes 1, 2, 3 and 4. Because the I chord is where the music usually starts and ends, it's called the CHORD OF RESOLUTION.

I Cross Harp Chord of Resolution
1234 Draw

The IV chord can be played by blowing on holes 1, 2, 3 and 4. The IV chord moves the music away from the Chord of Resolution. It's called the STEPPING STONE CHORD.

IV Cross Harp Stepping Stone Chord
1234 Blow

The V chord can be played by drawing on holes 4 and 5. The V chord creates musical tension, and is called the DOMINANT WAILER CHORD.

V Cross Harp Dominant Wailer Chord
45 Draw

To play a simple I-IV-V chord progression, begin stomping your foot 1-2-1-2.* Once you've got a beat going, play the Cross Harp Chord of Resolution for two stomps. Play the Stepping Stone Chord for two stomps. Play the Dominant Wailer Chord for two stomps. Complete your blues cycle by returning to the Chord of Resolution. Then play the cycle again.

Want to Sound More Musical?

Start a stomach tremble, a vibration from deep in your body that gives your breath and harmonica sound a pulse. Think of this as a tremolo or vibrato—a soft vibrating pressure from your gut. This vibrato can go soft or hard, slow or fast. At first, it's easier on the blow, but soon this tremolo will be a part of how you play.

---

* How fast should you stomp? Try pulse speed. Place your thumb on the big vein of your wrist. Feel the rhythm of your heartbeat. The first beat is 1, the second is 2, the third is 1 and so on. Start stomping at the same speed. Other ideas are to use a metronome or drum machine.

I-IV-V Beginner's Cycle

(1234)   1234   (45)   (1234)
Resolution   Stepping   Wailing   Resolution
I   IV   V   I

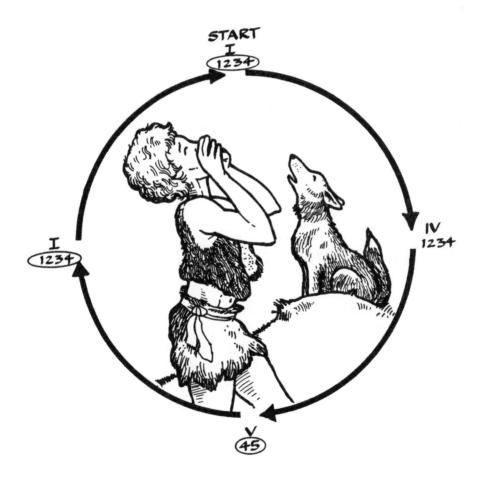

START
I
(1234)

IV
1234

I
(1234)

V
(45)

You can add rhythm and meaning by tonguing every chord twice.

44

You can change the order of chords in a I-IV-V progression. The next chord cycle plays the Dominant Wailer V Chord BEFORE the Stepping Stone IV Chord.

Foot Stomper's Cycle

(1234) 　　　　 (45) 　　　　 1234 　　　　 (1234)
Resolution 　 Wailing 　　 Stepping 　 Resolution
I 　　　　　　 V 　　　　　 IV 　　　　　 I

After you've played the above chord cycle a few times without tonguing, tongue every chord three times each time you bring your foot down (this is called a triplet). Not tonguing the final Chord of Resolution will add to the sense of completion.

The next chord cycle starts on the Dominant Wailer and ends on the Chord of Resolution.

Dancing Dog Cycle

(45)   (1234)   1234   (1234)
Wailer   Resolution   Stepping   Resolution
V   I   IV   I

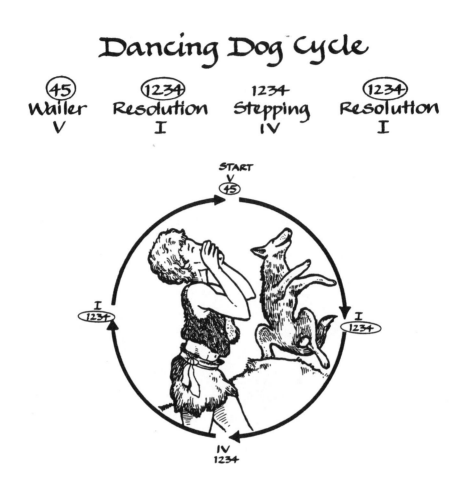

A suggestion for putting rhythm in the above cycle is to tongue every chord twice. Tonguing the final Chord of Resolution three times will add still more pzazzz.

Get a rhythm going and play these chords over and over. Stomp your foot 1-2-1-2-1-2. Play harp as you march around the house. Clap your hands as you clench your harp in your teeth. Do anything that will help you return to that ancient cave of your mind and that subterranean river where music and rhythm flow.

In other words, get it on!

46

The Sensuous Single Note

Although Stone was a rough and tumble Cave Boy, he had his sensuous side. But Stone had a problem. He couldn't run around being sensuous with everybody he met; he'd be arrested. So Stone learned to convey his sensuality through the harmonica.

This sensuous approach was most important when playing a single note: playing one note at a time. It was as though he treated the harmonica as a person, a person he cared about. The result was a rich, clear single note that would do anything he asked it to.

Now it's your turn to play a single note. Before you sits your harmonica. "Play me," it says, "Pick me up and play a sweet single note."

Being the obedient type (especially when it comes to your harmonica) you place your little friend to your puckered lips. You blow through hole number 3, and play a clear single note.

"Ahhhh..." moans your harmonica. "It feels so good when you massage my reeds. And I love the way you pucker."

Indeed. Your lips are pushed out, well over the silver plates of your harmonica. Your tongue rests on the bottom of your mouth. Your airstream is gentle but persuasive as it guides a sweet 3 blow out of the harp and into the atmosphere.

"Play the Beginner's Blues Riff," says the harp. "You can do it."

Slowly, you move the harmonica about a quarter inch to the right and DRAW on hole 4.

"Yes!"cries the harp. "Four draw. But I do need a feeling of musical tension. Tongue me. Please."

As you draw on hole 4, you tap the tip of your tongue on the fleshy ridge behind your upper teeth. *Ta ta ta. Ta ta ta.* The flicking tip of your tongue punctuates the wailing 4 draw. Musical tension builds as this important blues harmonica note belts out phrases the same way a singer belts out words.

④
"My baby left me this morning!"
Ta tata   ta   ta   ta

You swivel your harp from the 4 draw back to the 3 blow. Your tongue taps out the singer's phrasing of:

3
"I don't know what to do!"
Ta ta   ta   ta   ta ta

The voice of your harp is pure and rich. The punctuation of your tongue gives meaning and feeling to the 3 blow and the 4 draw.

And your harp? "Mmmmmmmmmm" it says, "you sure know how to play single notes. Especially for someone just starting out."

○ means draw

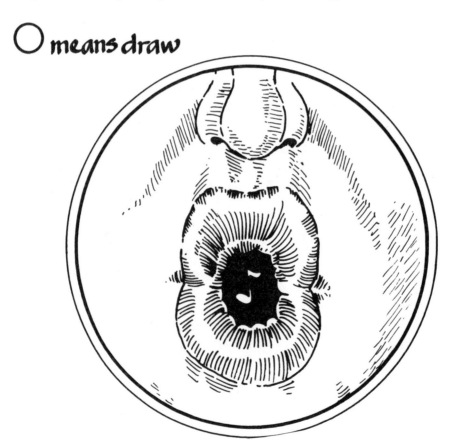

The Practical Single Note

Decide which note you want to play, line it up to your puckered lips, and kiss that harp. The trick is in the pucker. Push your lips out so they form a vertical oval – a tongue moistened gateway that's higher than it is wide. Now, PLAY THAT NOTE.

Some tips:

1. Practice your single notes for 8, 12 or 16 beats so you have a chance to hear and improve them.

2. Don't hold your harp on the edges of your lips. The further in your mouth you can put your harp, the richer will be your tone.

3. Don't press your upper lip down on the harp. Don't make it stretch or reach for the harp. Move the harp and your puckered mouthpiece *up* towards your nose. Rest your upper lip on the top plate of the harp.

4. Make your single note hole as big as possible. Make your lips big and flabby feeling. Don't puff out your cheeks.

5. Blow and draw smooth, round airstreams from and to top of your throat and nasal passages. This is called playing from your head. Do everything gently and smoothly. Play softly, but firmly. Control your air.

6. Think of an air tunnel that starts where your lips pucker around the harp and goes to the top of your head and down into your voice box and stomach. Let the air flow freely through this tunnel.

7. Give the airstream a start and stop stutter effect by tonguing.

8. If you start to hear part of another note along with your single note, pucker more.

9. If you have trouble finding the note you want, mark it with a piece of tape on your harmonica.

10. When searching for a note, don't pull your harp out of your mouth. Rather, slide the harp sideways between your moistened lips. Continue blowing or drawing as you slide.

11. Be patient. Listen to your single note. The more you relax, the better it will sound. Clear single notes are the keys to good harp playing.

Final Words for Chapter Two

By now you should be exploring the sounds of your harmonica with great fervor. Some of these noises will sound great; others terrible. The important thing is to feel relaxed with your harmonica, to not try *too* hard.

Continue blowing and drawing as you read through Chapters II, III, IV, V and beyond. Soon your chords, single notes, and ability to play to a beat will come into their own.

Until then, be patient, spontaneous, and most important, have fun.

Notes

* To play blues, rock or country harmonica, you need a small, ten-holed diatonic harmonica.

* The most frequently used keys are **A, C, D, F** and **G.**

* The different keyed harmonicas are organized exactly the same. If you can play a song or "riff" on a **C** harp, you can play the same song on any other key of harmonica. This is the PRINCIPLE OF HARMONICA RELATIVITY.

* Make the first sounds on your harmonica relaxed and easy.

* Put RHYTHM into your sounds by TONGUING, tapping the tip of your tongue behind your upper teeth as in *ta ta ta*.

* Throughout this book, a circled number means DRAW. An uncircled number means BLOW.

* To play a I-IV-V CHORD PROGRESSION, make 1234 draw your I chord, 1234 blow your IV chord, and play your V chord by drawing on holes 4 and 5. Be sure to resolve on 1234 draw.

* Playing clear SINGLE NOTES is essential to playing sensuous harmonica. Practice on 3 blow and 4 draw.

THREE

Cross Harp: Sound of the Blues

*Cross Harp is the style of harmonica that plays the blues. It involves accenting the draw notes instead of the blow notes and playing a **C** harmonica in the key of **G**. Chapter III will introduce you to Cross Harp and get you started making those wailing blues sounds.*

First Position Straight Harp: Playing <u>C</u> Harp in the Key of <u>C</u>

One reason Stone became so intimate with his boo boo tree **C** harp was that he could play it anytime, anywhere.

For instance, he could play while taking a bath in the steamy hot pools behind his cave. The sounds he'd make would echo off the rock canyon walls, flowing like water itself. Or, the fledgling cave boy might play while walking along the streets of Cave City, huffing and puffing a draw blow rhythm to some primitive variation of the I-IV-V progression.

From all this playing, Stone discovered two basic harmonica styles: STRAIGHT HARP. and CROSS HARP. Straight Harp, which accented the BLOW notes, worked best for playing melodies. Cross Harp, stressing the draw notes, produced a sweet, bluesy sound that created and resolved tension, used Adam's 1-2½-4-5-6½-1 Blues Scale, and made it impossible for people hearing it to feel lonely or out of sorts.

Remembering that music is made up of harmonizing notes and chords (as well as rhythm and soul), here's a good way to understand Straight Harp.

On your **C** harmonica, blowing on holes 1234 at the same time produces a **C** chord. Higher **C** chords can be played by blowing on holes 4567 or 789 and 10. These are the Straight Harp Blow Chords.

Playing your harmonica in a way that accents the 1-3-5 harmonizing notes that make up each of these **C** chords allows you to play your **C** harmonica in the key of **C**. This is Straight Harp.

This is where these Straight Harp harmonizing notes are located.

Straight Harp Harmonizing Notes

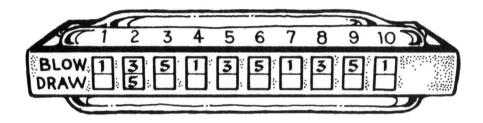

Notice that *every* blow note is a harmonizer. Some are the 1st note of the **C** scale. Others are the 3rd or 5th note. And remember: when accompanying a I-IV-V chord progression being played on piano, guitar (or iced tea glasses), the harmonizing notes will always sound good – no matter what phase of the music the chord progression the music is in.

So, to play Straight Harp, accent the BLOW notes. Use the draw non-harmonizing notes as stepping stones between one harmonizer and the next.

Chapter VIII explains Straight Harp in greater detail. Chapter IX presents simple Straight Harp songs you can learn to play. For now, move up and down your harmonica, blowing and drawing, accenting the blows. To accent a note, play it longer, louder and with more feeling.

Finally, end your Straight Harp jam by blowing on holes 1234 or any other Straight Harp Blow Chord. That's how you play a **C** harp in the key of **C**.

---

* No need to memorize this. Just notice that every blow note is a harmonizer.

Second Position Cross Harp: Playing <u>C</u> Harp in the Key of <u>G</u>

Cross Harp is the bluesy, get-down, gutsy, sexy style of harmonica that plays blues, rock and country western. This is the style that the streets of Cave City seemed to bring out of Stone. It's the style that eventually made the Cave Boy harpist famous. Here's how it works:

When you DRAW on holes 1234 of your **C** harp, you play a **G** chord.

Cross Harp Draw Chord

Accenting the harmonizing notes (and the blues harmonizing notes) that make up this Cross Harp Draw Chord is how you play your **C** harmonica in the key of **G**.

This is where the Cross Harp harmonizing notes are located:

Cross Harp Harmonizers

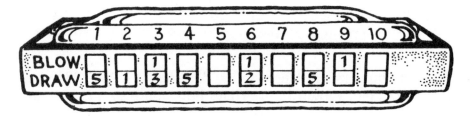

To play primitive Cross Harp, move up and down your harmonica, drawing and blowing, accenting the draws. End your jam on the Cross Harp Draw Chord.

Now that's the blues!

Musical Tension

Stone had a slightly more sophisticated approach to playing Cross Harp. He would create and resolve musical tension. To start, he'd establish home base for the sounds he was going to make. If the music were in the key of **G**, his home base would be a **G** note.

After tonguing out a rhythm on this home base, Stone would blow and draw his way up or down the harmonica to a blues harmonizing note – usually the 2nd, 2½ or 5th notes of Adam's Blues Scale. The harmonizer would sound terrific, but because it was away from home, it created a sense of TENSION. It *wailed*.

Then, when the moment felt right (depending on the timing of the music and the mood he wanted to create), Stone would draw and blow his way back to home base, RESOLVING the tension.

The result would be a feeling that the music had gone somewhere and returned, that the notes of Stone's harmonica had told a story – and that the story had a complete, satisfactory ending.

The notes that resolved the tension, the home base notes, were called NOTES OF RESOLUTION. These notes are 2 draw and 3 blow (which are the same note), 6 blow and 9 blow.

Cross Harp Notes of Resolution
2 Draw, 3 Blow, 6 Blow, 9 Blow

Notes of Resolution are the 1st note of the scale of the key you are playing in. When you play a **C** harp in the key of **G**, your Notes of Resolution are the **G** notes on this **C** harp.

The notes that created tension were called WAILING NOTES. These were the harmonizing notes and blues harmonizing notes of the Cross Harp Draw Chord. They were all played on the draw.

Cross Harp Wailing Notes
1 Draw, 3 Draw, 4 Draw, 6 Draw, 8 Draw

Accompanying a I-IV-V chord progression, Notes of Resolution and Wailing Notes will always harmonize with the music. Be sure you're playing the right key of harmonica and toot along on 3 blow (a Note of Resolution) or 4 draw (a Wailer). Grunt a lot. Wear dark glasses. Your friends will be amazed you've become a harp player so quickly.

If you don't want them to know you've only been playing harp for twenty minutes, avoid accenting the non-harmonizing notes. These non-harmonizers are mostly blow notes and are used as stepping stones between one harmonizer and the next. This is why they are called Stepping Stone Notes.

Stepping Stone Notes will sometimes harmonize when accompanying a I-IV-V chord progression, but not always. On the harmonica below, Cross Harp Wailing Notes and Notes of Resolution are portrayed in black and Stepping Stone Notes expressed in white.

---

* As explained in Chapter VII, 3 draw does not sound bluesy unless it is "bent". Bending is a technique that lets you lower the tone of the note by drawing the air *down* into your voice box. Three draw unbent is the 3rd note of the scale. Three draw bent is Adam's 2½ Blues Harmonizing Note.

Map of Cross Harp

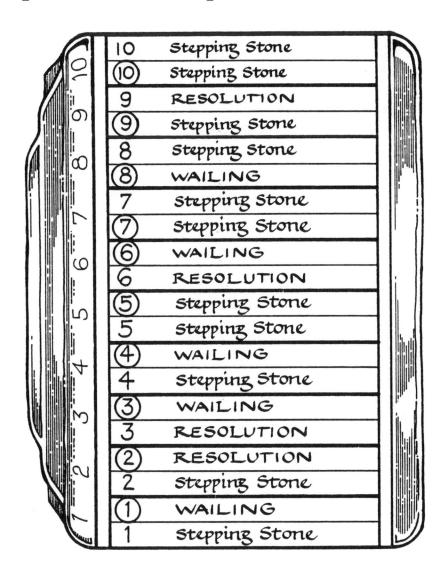

10	Stepping Stone
(10)	Stepping Stone
9	RESOLUTION
(9)	Stepping Stone
8	Stepping Stone
(8)	WAILING
7	Stepping Stone
(7)	Stepping Stone
(6)	WAILING
6	RESOLUTION
(5)	Stepping Stone
5	Stepping Stone
(4)	WAILING
4	Stepping Stone
(3)	WAILING
3	RESOLUTION
(2)	RESOLUTION
2	Stepping Stone
(1)	WAILING
1	Stepping Stone

NOTES OF RESOLUTION are home base. They are harmonizers, the 1st note of the scale of the key you're playing in.

WAILING NOTES create musical tension. They are blues harmonizers, the 2nd, 2½, 3rd and 5th notes of the scale.

STEPPING STONE NOTES *don't* always harmonize, though sometimes they sound great. Use them as steps between resolution and tension.

Cross Harp Boogie

Tap out a 3 blow on your harp. Stomp your foot and loosen up. That's right....

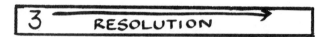

Now move that harp a tiny bit and draw on hole 4. Tongue that baby. Create a little tension. Hold that note as you stomp 1-2-1-2-1-2.

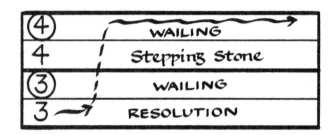

Now pause. *Feel* the tension you've created. Dig the silence. Now, and only now, play your Note of Resolution, 3 blow.

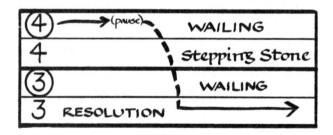

Oh yeah! Establish home base. Create tension. Resolve tension. Stomp your foot. Get down. Do it again. Whew! Play a lonnnnnnng 4 draw to the 1-2-1-2 beat.

Now, blow on hole 4, draw on 3 and resolve on 3 blow.

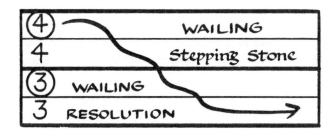

What a sound! *Stress* those harmonizing notes. Glide over those Stepping Stones.

Tongue that 3 blow. Create tension on 3 draw. Resolve on 3 blow. Keep your rhythm going....

Play a long, wailing 6 draw. *Ta ta ta, ta ta ta, ta ta ta.*

Resolve your tension on 6 blow.

Oh yeah! Get down and loosen up! You've got the blues in your shoes. Play 'em.

The Cross Harp Formula

The Cross Harp formula is a simple way to choose the correct key harmonica when playing Cross Harp to accompany a guitarist or piano player.

Ask the guitarist what key the song is in. If the answer is **G**, count up four steps (including the **G**)...

$$
\begin{array}{cccc}
G & A & B & C \\
1 & 2 & 3 & 4
\end{array}
$$

...and play your **C** harp in the key of **G**.

Likewise, if you have a **C** harp, and want to tell the guitarist what key to play in, count *back* four steps from the **C**. (It's okay to use your fingers!)

$$
\begin{array}{cccc}
G & A & B & C \\
4 & 3 & 2 & 1
\end{array}
$$

Here is a chart that tells you which harmonica you need to play Cross Harp in each of music's twelve different keys.

Musical Key	Key of Harp for Cross Harp
A flat	D flat
A	D
B flat	E flat
B	E
C	F
D flat	F sharp
D	G
E flat	A flat
E	A
F	B flat
F sharp	B
G	C

HOW TO FIGURE THE CROSS HARP FORMULA.

Notes

* There are two basic styles of harmonica playing: STRAIGHT HARP and CROSS HARP.

* Straight Harp accents the blow notes. When you play your **C** harmonica in the key of **C**, you are playing Straight Harp. Straight Harp works best for melodic harmonica.

* Cross Harp emphasizes the harmonica's draw notes. This blues harmonica style lets you play your **C** harmonica in the key of **G**.

* There are two kinds of notes on your harmonica: HARMONIZING NOTES and STEPPING STONES. Accompanying a I-IV-V chord progression, harmonizing notes will never make a mistake – no matter where in the progression they are played.

* There are two kinds of harmonizing notes: WAILING NOTES and NOTES OF RESOLUTION. Notes of Resolution establish home base and resolve tension. Wailing Notes move the music away from home base and create tension.

* To play bluesy patterns of notes (also known as riffs, runs, and licks), emphasize Wailing Notes and Notes of Resolution. Use non-harmonizing Stepping Stone Notes as links between these Wailers and Resolvers.

* To figure out which key of harmonica to use when playing Cross Harp, find out what key the music is in. If the music you're accompanying is in, say, the key of **A** count up four steps...

A B C D
1 2 3 4

...and play a **D** harp.

FOUR

Cave Jam: How to Accompany

Travel back 10,000 years to that musty cave where The Cave Boys are laying down some good tunes. Bring your harmonica and play some simple accompaniment. Hey, you play pretty good!

Cave Jam

It was a large, comfortable cave high in the hills above a broad valley. This was where the Cave Boys practiced. The sounds of their instruments would echo loudly off the cave walls. But because the cave was far away from the homes of other cave men, there were few complaints about noise.

It was Sunday afternoon, and the Cave Boys were getting ready to play. This was a new song, written by Krok, the band's lead guitar player and singer. The song was in the key of **G**. *

Counting up four steps, **G** (1) **A** (2) **B** (3) **C** (4), Stone was prepared to boogie on his **C** harp.

Krok's fingers formed a **G** chord on his guitar. "You guys ready?" he asked.

"Yeah," said the big drummer, Smash.

Gref, the bass player, nodded. Stone softly tapped his **C** harp in the palm of his hand.

"Okay," said Krok, "One-two-three-four!"

Whang bam thump thump!! The I-IV-V chord progression started with 4 beats in the chord of **G**. This was the I Chord of Resolution.

As the fourth beat came down, Krok swung his guitar low across his body and changed his **G** chord to a chord in the key of **C**. This was the IV Stepping Stone Chord and the music stayed here for 4 beats. *Whamma bam bam!* slammed the drums as the music returned to the **G**, this time for 8 beats.

"Yeah!" shouted Smash, big arms flailing as he pounded his cymbals and snare drums.

Krok's long fingers danced to the **C** chord for 8 beats and returned to the **G** chord for 8 more.

Here in the **G**, the chord progression seemed to be asking for a change, and a change is what it got. The Cave Boy guitarist nodded to his bass player, jumped lightly from the dirt cave floor, and played a **D** chord, the Dominant Wailer V Chord of the I-IV-V chord progression. This **D** chord gave the music a feeling of movement, of going somewhere. The **D** lasted 4 beats. Then the chord cycle swung down to the **C** chord for 4 tense beats. Oh yeah!

Krok slammed out the **G** chord as the blues cycle came home to the I Chord of Resolution. Four beats passed and the cycle was almost complete. But what's this? With only 4 beats left in the blues cycle, Krok returned to his Dominant Wailer, the **D** chord.

"Turn it around!" shouted Smash. The tension wailed for one-two-three-four beats – and at exactly the right moment, the music dove home to the **G** chord for a dramatic resolution of the old cycle and the start of a new one.

This was the TWELVE BAR BLUES CYCLE, a special I-IV-V chord progression that even today is almost always heard when a band plays the slow blues. But Krok didn't care about that. He wanted to hear his harp player. "C'mon Stonie boy," he shouted.   "C'mon!"

Stone began by playing Wailing Note 4 draw. As the I-IV-V chord progression moved through its cycle, each chord change gave the 4 draw new meaning and feeling – almost as though he were changing notes. Because this wailing 4 draw was a harmonizing note, it never made a mistake.

Then, as the cycle neared resolution (and Stone's lungs were about to explode), the fiesty harp player went to the Note of Resolution, 3

68

blow. The 3 blow and the I Chord of Resolution hit at exactly the same time. Wow!

Now, as the cycle started around again, Stone tongued his 3 blow Note of Resolution, *beating* a rhythm, *phrasing* his sounds the way a singer phrases words. Stone tongued this 3 blow through the entire cycle.

As the cycle started up once more, Stone began playing other Cross Harp harmonizing notes. He played the 6 draw Wailer. He took a run up to the 9 blow Note of Resolution and played his harp down, curling over the notes to Note of Resolution 3 blow. Because he accented the Notes of Resolution and Wailing Notes and played the Stepping Stone Notes lightly, like rungs on a ladder between the harmonizers, he never made a mistake.

"Alright!" shouted Krok as the cycle came to a close. The guitarist opened his mouth wide and started to sing. He might not have had the best voice in the world, but when it came to grunting, groaning, moaning and screaming, no one did it better.

G *(guitar chords)*   **C**
"I've got the Cave Boy Blues, and wouldn't it be fine?"

G
(Stone tongued his 3 blow for 8 beats)

C
"I've got the Cave Boy blues, and wouldn't it be fine?"
G
(Stone played 3 blow, moved to 4 draw and wailed for 8 beats)

D   **C**   **G**
"If you'd pay a little visit to Krokie boy's cave sometime."
G   **D**   **G**
(Stone tongued 3 blow, wailed on 4 draw, slid up to 6 draw, re-solved on 6 blow)

"Alright!" shouted Krok, sounding a little like a man with his leg caught in a meat grinder.

Now Stone played a solo of low notes. He drew and tongued hole number one. He blew on hole two and sucked a clear single note on Note of Resolution 2 draw.

His 2 draw slipped up to 3 draw. By changing the shape of his mouth and throat, Stone sucked that note deep into his gut. The 3 draw dipped down to a "bent" 3 draw.* This was the 2½ blues harmonizing note discovered by Adam. It sounded soooo good.

The blues cycle was coming around to the Dominant Wailer. Stone jumped up to holes 4 and 5 draw. These were the tension creating Wailing Notes, the single note expressions of the V Dominant Wailer Chord. Stone swivelled his harmonica back and forth between 4 and 5 draw without stopping his breath.

He continued this 4 and 5 single note draw slide through the IV chord, slipping the harp back and forth like a typewriter carriage between moist Cave Boy lips. It was a small subtle move, but what a sound it made!

Then, as the cycle came home, Stone came home to the 6 blow Note of Resolution. He played 6 draw as the cycle turned around with the Dominant Wailer V Chord, and blew home with a wild flurry of notes that somehow landed on the 3 blow at exactly the same moment that Krok dropped to his knees, clutched his guitar to his chest, and started to sing:

G   **C**
"I've got the Cave Boy blues, and wouldn't it be great?"

G
(Stone drew a long 3 draw bent down for 7 beats and played 3 blow on the 8th beat)

C
"I've got the Cave Boy blues and wouldn't it be great?"

---

* More about bending in Chapter VII

G
(Stone played 1 draw, 2 blow, 2 draw and made that 2 draw talk
until the 8th beat)

D   **C**   **G**
"If you'd consent to be this cave boy's date."

G   **D**   **G**
(Stone played 4 draw, 4 blow, 3 draw, 4 blow, 3 draw, 2 draw)

Stone caressed home his 2 draw Note of Resolution and took off
on a new solo. Smash double thumped his drums and Gref's low
bass notes drove home a deep blues feeling. Round and round went
the I-IV-V chord progression, this twelve bar blues cycle.
Stone's harmonica growled like a wildcat, howled like a coyote,
moaned like a lover who wanted more. It was incredible.

Stone even played the Six Blow Down, a harp riff using Adam's
Blues Scale – only in reverse. Note of Resolution 6 blow was the 1st
note. Five draw was the $6\frac{1}{2}$ note. Four draw served as the wailing
5th note. Four blow was the 4th note. Three draw bent down was
the $2\frac{1}{2}$ blues harmonizing note, and 3 blow, another Note of
Resolution, was the 1st note of the scale.

Blues Scale Down

6 ⑤④ 4 ③ 3

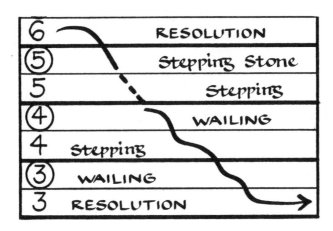

71

As the music swelled and reverberated off the musty walls, the other band members just looked at each other. Stone's music sounded so good it was hard to concentrate.

How could he do all that on a tiny harmonica?

Finally, Krok could stand it no longer. He put his guitar down, unplugged it from his electric tree stump. "Tell me…" he gasped, "Tell me…how did you do that?"

Stone smiled. "What key is the next song in?" Then he turned away and acted busy. A harp player never reveals his or her secrets – unless there's cash involved.

Finally, Stone agreed to teach the Cave Boys how to play Cross Harp for 20 clams a person. Fresh, *plump* clams. And he'd even let them use his harps.

Notes

* Music moves in circles. The circle almost always plays the same chord pattern again and again. This is a CHORD PROGRESSION. Most chord progressions are built around the I-IV-V pattern.

* To jam with a band, guitarist, or a record, find out where the music begins and ends. This is the KEY you're playing in.

* Select the CORRECT KEY HARMONICA. To play Cross Harp, count up 4 steps from the key the music is in. If the music is in the key of **G**, play a **C** harp. If the music is in the key of **E**, play an **A** harp.

* Get a FEEL for the music before you start your accompaniment. Let the rhythm flow through your body. Get a sense of the chord progression's circular motion.

* A good way to START YOUR ACCOMPANIMENT is to play a long 4 draw. Hear how each chord change gives new meaning and feeling to this harmonizing note.

* GO SLOW AND HAVE A GOOD TIME.

FIVE

Stone's Harmonica Lesson: Blues and Rock Riffs

Riffs are patterns of notes that always sound bluesy and musical. They connect Notes of Resolution, Wailing Notes and Stepping Stone Notes to help you make music as you blow and draw your way around the harmonica. Some of the riffs in Chapter V are too difficult to play immediately. Don't let this stop you from tooting along and having a good time.

The Lesson Begins

Stone told the Cave Boys how Wailing Notes create musical tension and Notes of Resolution resolve tension. He told them how Stepping Stone Notes were used as links, or rungs on a ladder, between Wailing Notes and Notes of Resolution. Still, the band was impatient.

"Okay," growled Smash, "Now we know which notes create tension and which notes resolve it. What are we supposed to do? Play them all at the same time?"

"Take it easy," said Stone. "Let's take Wailing Note 4 draw and Note of Resolution 3 blow. We know you can play either one – and they'll always work when you accompany a I-IV-V chord progression." He picked up his harmonica and played the Beginner's Blues Riff.

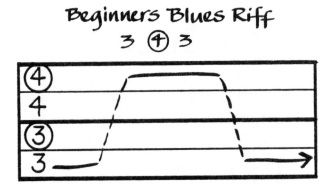

"If playing 3 blow and 4 draw always works, why not build a ladder, using 3 draw and 4 blow as Stepping Stones? Like this:"

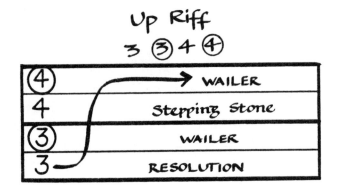

76

He handed each of the Cave Boys a small diatonic harmonica. "Now you guys try it...but don't spit too much in the harps. It clogs them up."

Each of the Cave Boys tried to play the Up Riff.

But instead of the smooth, rich tone Stone got from his harmonica, all the Cave Boys could produce was a cacophony of hisses, bleats, and honks.

It sounded like an invasion of geese.

"C'mon you guys," said Stone. "You gotta get a good single note before you can play a lick. You gotta pucker, like this..."

Stone pushed his lips out so they formed a verticle oval.

"...and see, you put the harmonica well inside your mouth. Push it up a little bit – towards your nose – so your upper lip doesn't have to stretch so much."

He looked at Smash, whose face was set in a determined grimace. "Smash!" he shouted.

But it was too late. Smash removed the harmonica from his mouth. It was crushed to smithereens – bent by the pressure of the big drummer's clenched lips.

"You gotta relax!" shouted Stone. "You gotta mellow out with those big lips of yours!"

He looked sadly at the crushed harmonica.

"Okay," he finally sighed. "Let's try again. Blow and draw on hole 3; blow and draw on hole 4. Remember, 4 draw is your Wailing Note, so play the 3 blow, 3 draw and 4 blow quickly and smoothly. Then, when you get to the 4 draw, stretch it out. Waaaaaiiiilllllllllll."

Once again the Cave Boys played the Up Riff. This time it sounded a lot better, though there were still many missed notes and strange honking sounds.

"That's a little better," said Stone. "But I don't see what's so hard about it. You blow and draw on 3. You blow and draw on 4, and you hold the 4 draw a long time to create tension."

The Cave Boys went at it again. Sure enough, they could hear the blues in this simple pattern of notes. In fact, a few of the times they tried it, even Stone was impressed. Of course, he didn't tell them.

Those crazy dudes might think they already know how to play harp. They might decide to forget about the lesson. And Stone could taste those clams.

The Down Riff

"Now that you're playing a riff that takes you up your harmonica, I'm gonna show you one that takes you down," said Stone. "All you've got to do is play the Up Riff in reverse. And dig it, you've got a hot blues lick."

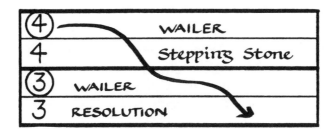

"That's it," Stone said as the Cave Boys played their own versions of the Down Riff.

"Now, 4 draw is a Wailing Note, so play it a long time. Maybe two beats, eh? The 4 blow is a Stepping Stone Note so play it quickly and move to the 3 draw. The 3 draw is a Wailer. You can really create tension with this little bugger, so hold it out. Try to create a sense of anticipation for the 3 blow. Then, after 2 or 3 beats (depending on how it feels best to you), play 3 blow."

"And the Down Riff is like the Up Riff? It will always sound good when accompanying a I-IV-V chord progression?" asked Krok.

"Of course," said Stone, "As long as it accents the Wailing Notes and Notes of Resolution."

"Prove it," said Krok. He picked up his guitar and began playing. His fingers leapt from chord to chord. First he played a **G** chord, then an **A** minor chord, then a **C** chord and lastly a **D**.

"Hey!" said Smash, "That's not a I-IV-V chord progression."

"It's close enough," said Stone. "As long as the music stays in the same key, these harmonica riffs will work. All you have to do is *mold* them to the music.

As Krok strummed the chords, Stone played the Down Riff as fast as he could, over and over. It fit perfectly with the music.

Then he played it very slowly, putting a big accent on the 3 draw Wailing Note. Again, it sounded great with guitar music.

Next, Stone played the Down Riff so the 4 draw lasted 12 beats, the 4 blow and 3 draw occurred in 1 beat and the resolving 3 blow was played for 3 beats.

Now Krok changed his chord progression. He stayed in the key of **G**, but his fingers jumped to the **F** chord, back to the **G**, to the **F**, back to the **G**. Then he went to the **E** minor chord, the **A** minor chord, to the **D** chord, and finally back to the **G** chord.

"Whew!" said Smash. But Stone kept right on playing the Down Riff. As he played the Cave Boys gradually realized that what Stone said was true. Any riff that puts the accent on a Wailing Note or Note of Resolution will sound terrific when accompanying a blues or rock n' roll chord progression.

"You see, boys," the harp player finally said, "These riffs aren't exact. They're basic moves you can make on your harp. But *how* you make the move depends on the music you're accompanying, and what feels best to you."

"But how do you know what riff to play next?" asked Smash.

"Dig it," Stone replied. "Playing harp is like being in a good conversation. You don't know what you're going to say next; and if you tried to plan it, you'd probably get tongue-tied.

"You'll learn the language. Then you let what comes out of your mouth be a complete surprise. You catch on to the flow and feeling of the music and trust yourself.

"And if you make a mistake, say, playing 5 draw instead of 4 draw, don't worry about it. Just incorporate the 5 draw into the music.

Invent your own blues lick."

"How?" asked Krok.

"Lots of ways. But the most obvious is by sliding back to the 4 draw and wailing. The result would be:

Five Draw Mistake

3 ③ 4 ⑤④

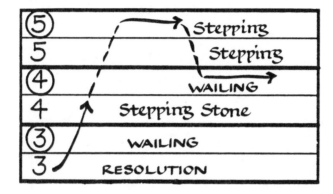

Stone played the 5 Draw Mistake.

"Hey, that's pretty good," said Smash. "I guess mistakes aren't really so bad after all."

"Not when you make them on purpose," winked Stone.

More Music on Holes
Three and Four

"In case you haven't noticed," said Stone, "Holes 3 and 4 are a veritable orchestra. There are so many patterns to play here that I couldn't begin to count them all.

"For instance, you can join the Up Riff and the Down Riff so they form one lick: the Up and Down Blues Riff."

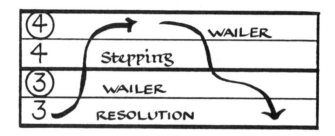

Up and Down Blues Riff
3 ③ 4 ④④ 4 ③ 3

"The Up and Down Blues Riff starts out on Note of Resolution 3 blow. The 3 blow lets you know where home base is, where the music starts and ends. Then you take the Up Riff to the 4 draw Wailing Note. Play this 4 draw a long time to create tension.

"Then (and this is important), you pause. End of the Up Riff. Enter the Down Riff. Four draw, 4 blow, now a long moan of a 3 draw that creates tension...and FINALLY your Note of Resolution 3 blow.

"Now you guys try it."

It was hard work teaching these Neanderthals to play Cross Harp. But one thing about cave men, they were willing to work hard. Thus, in a couple of hours, all the Cave Boys (even Smash, who paid an extra 5 clams for a new harp) were sounding pretty good on the Up and Down Riff.

Stone threw another piece of wood on the fire. Smoke billowed through the cave. "Okay," he coughed, "Now I'm going to show you guys some new licks and patterns on holes 3 and 4."

He squatted on the dirt floor of the cave and used a twig to draw some primitive diagrams.

"For instance, instead of playing 4 draw, 4 blow, 3 draw, 3 blow, play 4 draw, 4 blow, 3 draw, 4 *draw*. That's right. Instead of resolving tension, slide back to the 4 draw Wailer – and create tension."

Four Draw Surprise
④ 4 ③④

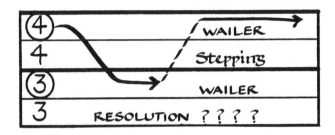

"You can play the 4 Draw Surprise over and over, and it will always fit in with the I-IV-V chord progression. Then, when you're tired of creating tension, finish your pattern with a 3 blow.

"And it sounds real good to alternate the 4 Draw Surprise with the Up Riff and the Down Riff. Like this..."

Stone put his harp to his mouth, puckered, and began to play in a clear, throbbing tone.

④ 4 ③ 3 (Down Riff)
④ 4 ③ ④ (4 Draw Surprise)
3 ③ 4 ④ (Up Riff)
④ 3 ③ 3 (Down Riff)

"Hey!" shouted Krok, "That sounds just like a little blues song!"

"Of course," said Stone. "That is because the first riff established home base, the next two riffs created tension, and the final riff returned to home base."

"And you did all that on two harmonica holes," said Smash. Thinking of the ton load of drums he had to carry around just to make a little music, he shook his head slowly.

"Maybe I've been playing the wrong instrument," he said.

"Careful," laughed Stone. "There's only one harp player in this band."

Two Draw

"Here's one of the best licks I know," said Stone. "I call it the Good Morning Riff because it sounds snappy and bright. It uses 2 draw as a Note of Resolution. Two draw is the same note as 3 blow. I find I use 2 draw when I'm playing a riff that comes from the bottom of the harp (such as the Good Morning Riff), and that I use the 3 blow Note of Resolution when I play a riff in the midrange of the harp (such as the Down Riff)."

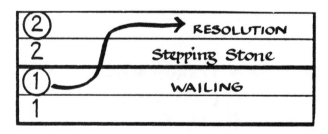

Stone played the Good Morning Riff a few times. Sure enough, it did sound snappy and bright. But when the Cave Boys tried, the riff sounded like it hadn't had a good night's sleep in weeks. The trouble was with the 2 draw. None of the beginning harp players could get a sound out of the rebellious note.

"What the heck's wrong with my 2 draw?" Smash asked. He peered angrily into the little square hole.

"The low draw notes give everyone trouble," Stone said. "The tendency is to tighten up when you suck on them. When they don't respond, the tendency is to suck even harder. Good way to break your harp.

"But if you want to play 2 draw right, try this. Take your harp out of your mouth. Now, rub your lips. Pinch them. Pucker up. Now relax...

"Consider, gentlemen, if you placed a straw up to that 2 draw and gently sucked, the note would play perfectly. But the way *you* go about playing the 2 draw Note of Resolution, forcing the air into your throat, you can't even get a sound. Hah!

"Put your harp back into your mouth, push it up towards your nose. Gently, very gently, draw a controlled stream of air to the roof of your mouth. *Coax* that note out. Keep the feeling light and airy. That note will come, but you gotta persuade it."

Armed with this new advice, the Cave Boys went to work on the 2 draw. Gref got it first – probably because he was a more relaxed type of guy. But before long, all the Cave Boys were playing the 2 draw, and the Good Morning Riff.

"Like any riff I show you," said Stone, "The Good Morning Riff can be played with many variations. Try tonguing the 2 draw in triplets: ① 2 ②(triplet).

"Or bounce back and forth between the 2 draw and the 2 blow: ① 2 ② 2 ②

"You also can use the Good Morning Riff as a starting place for a pattern that takes you up to 3 draw."

Good Morning Three Draw
① 2 ② ③

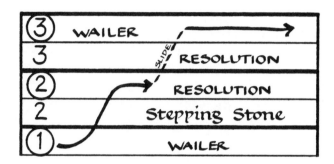

"Or, you can continue the riff up to 4 draw."

Good Morning Four Draw
① 2 ② ③ 4 ④

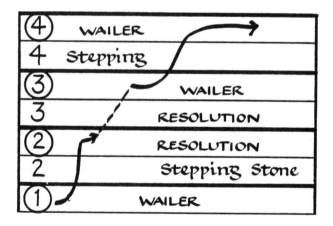

"But for simple accompaniment to a song you don't know that well, the Good Morning Riff ending on 2 draw: 1 draw, 2 blow, 2 draw – with a little tonguing action thrown in on the 2 draw is the safest way to go. Play it over and over, changing the timing and feeling to fit the music. It will never make a mistake."

Surprise Resolution

"If you've been paying attention," Stone said, "You've probably noticed that most of the Cross Harp riffs I've shown you are built around a Note of Resolution.

"The Up Riff, the Down Riff, the Four Draw Surprise – all use the 3 blow. The Good Morning Riff uses the 2 draw.

"Now I want to show you a couple of riffs that resolve on the 6 blow Note of Resolution. Six blow is the same note as 2 draw or 3 blow, but it's up an octave. (See page 16) You can toot along on 6 blow through an entire song and never make a mistake.

"The first riff we should try is the Surprise Resolution. It starts as though you were playing the Down Riff: 4 draw, 4 blow, 3 draw... but instead of resolving on 3 blow, slide the harp up to Note of Resolution 6 blow. Like this:

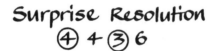

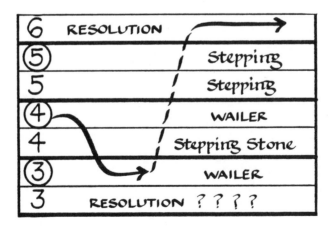

"Not bad," said Krok after he'd played the Surprise Resolution a few times. "It doesn't do what you'd expect, but it sounds good anyway. What else can you do with the 6 blow?"

"Why not go into the 6 draw?" suggested Gref. "I see here on your Cross Harp Map that it's a Wailing Note. Maybe I can create tension on the 6 draw and resolve it on the 6 blow."

Gref played a long cry on the 6 draw. Then, very gently, he brought it home to the Note of Resolution, 6 blow.

Six Draw and Blow Resolution
⑥ 6

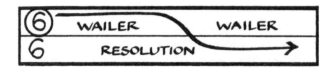

"That's really sweet," said Krok. "But here's an idea. Tongue the 6 draw to create even more tension."

The shaggy-haired guitarist put the harp in his mouth, puckered to get a clear single note, and drew on hole 6. Keeping one long draw, he tongued *ta ta taaaaaaa*.

Then, he stopped and looked at the rest of the Cave Boys with a sly smile.

"C'mon..." complained Smash.

"If you don't play that 6 blow, I will," said Gref.

Stone threw his head back and laughed. "Boy, that 6 draw sure created tension. I mean, it's still hanging there in the air. Somebody's got to resolve it."

"I can't stand it," Smash said. He played the 6 blow. There was a tremendous sense of release, of resolution, a feeling of being able to breathe again.

Krok looked at his harmonica in amazement. "Hey, this is a powerful little thing, isn't it?"

Good Old Six Blow

"Here's a nice little lick that will take you from Note of Resolution 6 Blow Down to Note of Resolution 3 blow," said Stone. "It's kinda like a scale:"

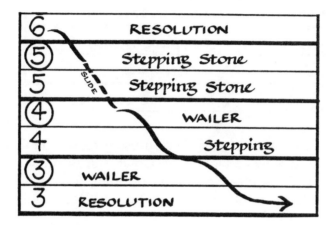

Six Blow Down
6 ⑤ ④ 4 ③ 3

Tapping his foot 1 – 2 – 1 – 2 Stone played the 6 Blow Down a few times. "Now, one of the tricks in playing this lick is the way you move the harp from 5 draw to 4 draw. You SLIDE the harp, continuing to draw. If you do it by drawing on hole 5, stopping the draw, moving the harp to hole 4, and starting your draw again, the riff will sound clumsy."

"See what you mean," said Gref after he slowly played the 6 Blow Down. "What do you call that?"

"A DRAW SLIDE," said Stone. "It's one of those little details that can make a huge difference. And heck, it's not hard to keep drawing as you move the harp. Sure improves your music, though."

---

* Six Blow Down is Adam's Blues Scale played in reverse.

The Cave Boys played with the 6 Blow Down for several minutes, stomping out a 1 – 2 – 1 – 2 rhythm and putting the riff into this rhythmic framework.

After everyone had the hang of it, Stone said, "Now another thing you can do is stop the riff on 4 draw and create tension."

Six Blow Down Wailer Riff
6 ⑤ ④

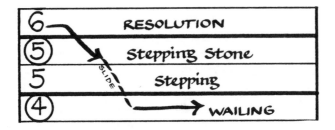

"And then you can resolve your tension using either the Good Morning Riff (1 draw, 2 blow, 3 blow), the Down Riff (4 draw, 4 blow, 3 draw, 3 blow), the Surprise Resolution (4 draw, 4 blow, 3 draw, 6 blow), or any other way of getting to a Note of Resolution you might discover."

"So tell me," said Gref, "When you play, do you think to yourself, 'Now I'm gonna play the Surprise Resolution, now I'm gonna create tension on 6 draw?' "

"I never do that," said Stone. "It would petrify me to play harp and think at the same time. No, playing harp is like dancing. You just blow and draw, warble and wail, and it comes out the way it's supposed to. And even if it isn't perfect, you still have a good time.

"And isn't that the whole point of playing music – to have a good time?"

"Then what's the purpose of learning all these riffs?" asked Smash. "Why not just pick the ol' harmonica up and play it?"

"I think you should," replied Stone. "When you practice, you should get your 1 – 2 – 1 – 2 beat going, try a few of the licks you've learned

90

from me, then leave those behind and play your own. After a few minutes of *not using* the stuff you've memorized, try the riffs again, always keeping your two stomp beat.

"By going back and forth between memorizing and being spontaneous, you'll be teaching yourself and having a good time. After a few days of working this way, the licks you've memorized will have become part of the way you pick the harp up and play it. They'll be natural. Know what I mean?"

Stone looked at his watch, a small Timex strapped to his wrist with dinosaur sinew. "Listen fellows, it's been hours. Haven't I earned my clams yet?"

"Is there more to the harmonica?" asked Krok.

"Well...of course," said Stone. "But it would take hours to cover everything: bending notes, how to use your hands, how to play these riffs in a I-IV-V blues cycle, using microphones, amplifiers, playing with records. Don't you think you've heard enough?"

"What about the notes above 6 draw?" Krok persisted.

"Well, they're a little more difficult than the notes on holes 1 through 6; but if you want to know about them, I'll tell you."

"If you want your clams," said Smash, "you'll tell us."

Nine Blow

Stone squatted in the dirt of the cave. The fire reflected dual images on his aviator glasses.

"Okay," he began. "Holes 1 through 6 are the nuts and bolts of simple Cross Harp. Still, the holes above 6 will add drama to your harp playing.

"When learning these high notes, it's a good idea to practice on your lower harps: **G, A** flat or **A**. Since these harps are pitched a little lower, the high notes aren't nearly as difficult to play."

Stone took an **A** harp from his harmonica bag and played a 9 blow.

Nine Blow

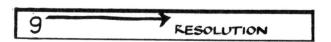

"Nine blow," he said, "is your Note of Resolution. It's the same note as 6 blow, only up an octave. It's the same note as 2 draw and 3 blow, but up two octaves." Stone gave **A** harps to Smash, Gref and Krok and let them work on the high, difficult 9 blow.

"Nine blow feels different than your lower notes," Stone said. "I change the shape of my lips and throat for this one. The airstream feels finely focused, and comes from my head rather than my throat or body as it does for the lower notes."

Nine blows (and pieces of 10 blows and 8 blows) screeched through the cave's musty air. "Takes a while to get the hang of this end of your harp," said Stone. "But it's worth it. There are some good licks up here."

"Such as?" asked Krok.

"Such as the 9 Blow Down," said Stone. "It takes you from the 9 blow Note of Resolution down to the 6 blow Note of Resolution. *

Stone cupped his hands around his harp and played a high, smooth lick starting on the 9 blow, lightly touching the 9 draw, the 8 blow, the 8 draw (creating a tiny bit of tension on this Wailing Note), sliding to the 7 draw, creating tension on the Wailing Note 6 draw and finally resolving on the 6 blow Note of Resolution.

"Remember," said Stone, "On holes 7 through 10, blow notes are higher than draw notes. Practicing the 9 Blow Down will help you get a feeling for this.

---

* Nine Blow Down is the same riff as 6 Blow Down, but is up an octave.

Nine Blow Down
9 ⑨ 8 ⑧ ⑦ ⑥ 6

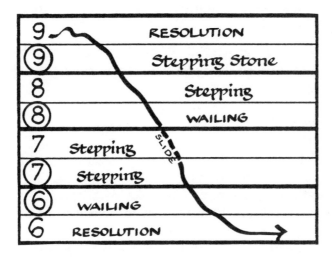

"Now, let me show you the 6 Blow Up. This is a Cross Harp lick that takes you from 6 blow to 9 blow.

Six Blow Up
6 ⑦⑧ 8 9

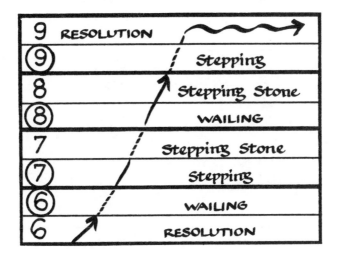

Each of the Cave Boy's attempted to play the 6 Blow Up, but the riff was difficult and frustrating – especially getting a clean sound on the 9 blow.

"How long did it take you to learn to play these high notes?" asked Gref.

"Man, I'm still learning," answered Stone. "Lots of times that 9 blow will just take off on me, or I'll try to play it and only get half the note. Sounds awful…"

"I've heard," said Krok.

Through his aviator glasses, Stone gave the lead guitarist a long, hard and dirty look. Even if he was a funky, harp-playing Cave Boy, Stone was a pretty sensitive guy. And, like most musicians, it was a lot easier for him to criticize himself than to hear it from others.

"Oh, yeah?" he finally said. He put his **A** harp to his lips. A long cry of a 9 blow rang out. Then the harp slid down over the notes, bending, twisting, shrieking, descending over the 9 draw, the 8 blow, the 8 draw, the 7 draw, the 6 draw, to the 6 blow, then performing a draw slide through the 5 draw, 4 draw, 3 draw, 2 draw, 1 draw- and back up through the 2 blow, 2 draw, 3 draw, and finally resolving on 2 draw.

"That, my friends, is the Complete Blues Scale Down."

Complete Blues Scale Down
9 ⑨ 8 ⑧⑦⑥ 6 ⑤④③②① 2 ②③②

10 - - -	Stepping WAILING When Bent
⑩	Stepping Stone
9	RESOLUTION
⑨	Stepping Stone
8	Stepping Stone
⑧	WAILING
7	Stepping
⑦	Stepping
⑥	WAILING
6	RESOLUTION
⑤	Stepping Stone
5	Stepping Stone
④	WAILING
4	Stepping Stone
③	WAILING
3	RESOLUTION
②	RESOLUTION
2	Stepping
①	WAILING
1	Stepping Stone

"And here," he said, "is the popular, amazing, and difficult-to-play Complete Blues Scale Up."

95

Complete Blues Scale Up

① 2 ② ③ 4 ④ 5 6 ⑦ ⑧ 8 9

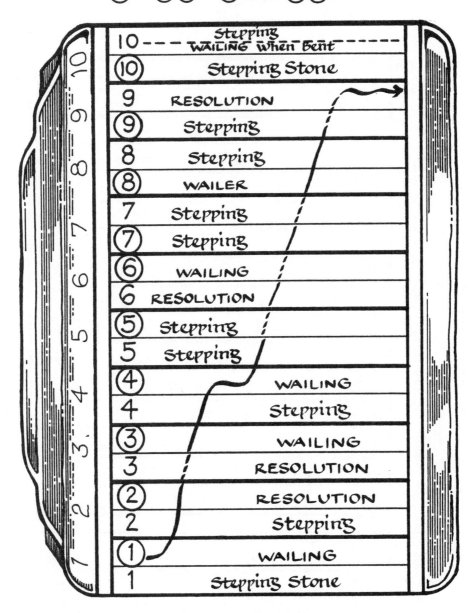

As Stone started on his 1 draw and moved swiftly and smoothly up the notes to 9 blow, Krok, Gref and Smash eyed each other. What was this guy trying to prove?

"Okay, Krok ol' boy," said Stone when the last echoes of the shrieking 9 blow had died. "It's your turn. Let's hear *you* play that lick."

"C'mon, man," said Krok. "I'm just starting out on harp. You know I can't play a lick like that."

"Don't have what it takes, eh?"

"Man, I play guitar…"

Stone laughed, "Not as difficult an instrument as harp, I guess."

"Listen, Stone…"

But Stone would not listen to Krok's excuses. Here he had spent hours showing these guys the secrets of Cross Harp, and Krok insults his playing.

"I'll bet you 20 clams you can't play this lick," Stone said.

Before Krok even had time to reply, Stone said, "I'll bet you *60* clams you can't play this lick."

Krok looked at the little harmonica resting in his hand. Its wooden edges and engraved hole numbers glistened in the firelight. He asked himself, could he play the Complete Blues Scale Up? Just once? Could he get lucky? Hmmmmmm 60 clams.

"Okay," he finally said. "You got a bet."

The Bet

Krok stood in the center of the cave. His face was streaked with sweat. His legs felt weak.

"Look," Gref said, "If you want to chicken out I'm sure Stone will…"

Krok hardly heard his worried bass player. He was deep inside himself, gathering his powers of concentration. Then, hands trembling, he cupped the boo boo reed beauty and put it to his puckered lips. Very softly, he played the 1 draw. A timid tone came from the harp. One draw. So far so good.

Knowing 1 draw was a Wailing Note, that he could play it as long as he wanted, Krok gently drew air through the reed inside the harp. (Since you know this same vital secret of Cross Harp, you might want to play your 1 draw as you read. It would give the story a nice musical backdrop.)

Now, from 1 draw, Krok would have to hop lightly to Stepping Stone 2 blow before he could find another safe spot. This would be Note of Resolution 2 draw.

$$\textcircled{1}\ 2\ \textcircled{2}$$

He mentally rehearsed this small move of his harmonica and the draw-blow-draw transition required to get to the Note of Resolution. Okay, he finally said to himself, let's do it.

He moved the harmonica to hole 2. He blew and then he sucked. Two draw rang through. He made it. He was safe. For now.

As he drew on Note of Resolution 2 draw, he planned his next move. From the 2 draw, he'd have to go to 3 draw, continue on to hole 4, blow, and immediately draw – ending up, theoretically, on Wailing Note 4 draw. Another safe spot that would always work.

$$\textcircled{2}\,\textcircled{3}\ 4\ \textcircled{4}$$

Okay. He was going for it. Carefully, he slid the harp from the 2 draw to the 3 draw. Being a Wailing Note (usually used as a Stepping Stone in this lick), the 3 draw gave him time to think.

Yeah, the voice in his head told him, move the harp to hole 4 at the same time that you blow. Then draw. Yeah, Krok, you can do it. With a gentle pull he moved the harp to hole 4 as he blew and sucked. Perfect! He was playing the 4 draw. No one thought he'd make it to 2 draw and here he was, wailing on the 4 draw. He opened his eyes and looked across the firelit cave where Stone watched through flame-licked aviator glasses. What Krok would give to read his mind now.

Ta ta ta. He flicked his tongue on the fleshy ridge behind his teeth as he drew the 4 draw reed. *Ta ta ta*.

Might as well create a little tension while I'm here, he said to himself. *Ta ta ta*.

Ah, but this was no time for messing around. He had to think. (And if thinking is tough for 20th Century man, consider what it must have been like for a Cave Boy.)

Now, this next move would not be as difficult. All he would have to do is move the harp to hole 5 and blow. Still blowing, he'd continue moving the harp to hole 6. And there he'd be – playing the 6 blow Note of Resolution.

④*5 6*

This is it, he thought. Gently he moved the harp to hole 5 and blew. Without breaking stride, he slid the harmonica to hole 6.

And there he was on 6 blow. *Ta ta ta*. His tongue tapped triumphantly on the moist ridge of his mouth just above his upper teeth. *Ta ta tatty ta taaaaah!*

What now?

Okay, he thought. First off, remember that the order of notes above 6 draw is reversed. From now on, blows are going to be higher than draws.

As for the move itself, it really didn't look that difficult. From the 6 blow Note of Resolution, slide the harp to hole 7 and draw. Continue sliding the harp to 8 draw.

6⑦⑧

Eight draw wasn't the most effective Wailing Note on the harp, but it would do for now. It would *have* to.

Bonzai, Cave Boy...

From the 6 blow, he sucked and moved the harp to hole 7 and to hole 8. Made it. But there was no time for congratulations. Eight draw just didn't sound that good as a Wailing Note.

But he was almost home. Almost 60 clams richer. All he'd have to do now was blow on hole 8 and blow on 9. Yeah. Go for it!

⑧ 8 9

So he did. He blew on the 8 and slid the harp to the 9. There he was – playing the 9 blow Note of Resolution. He had done it. He had actually played the Complete Blues Scale Up!

Still playing the 9 blow (wanting to savor the moment), Krok looked across the cave at Stone. To his surprise, the wirey harp player was smiling broadly. Hmmmmm, thought Krok, maybe Stone isn't such a bad guy after all.

"Yeah, man!" shouted Smash. He looked down at the tiny harmonica almost lost in his huge hand. If Krok could do it, so could he. The trick was to go real slow and to rest on the Wailing Note and Notes of Resolution.

"Right on," said Gref. He, too, was looking excitedly at his harmonica.

Ta ta ta! cried Krok's 9 blow. He made the note crow like a rooster, bark like a dog, wail like a fire engine. *Ta ta tatty ta taaaaah!* The triumphant 9 blow bounced and echoed off the cave walls. To all the Cave Boys, even Stone, the sound of this Note of Resolution was a thing of great beauty, a symbol of man's conquest over the unknown, a tribute to his ability to learn new skills.

Krok lowered the harp from his lips and smiled. Then he collapsed to the cave floor. Poor guy hadn't taken a decent breath in what seemed like hours.

~~~

If you've been playing along while reading, be certain you breathe once in a while. And if you *have* been having trouble with your breathing, The Sensuous Harp Player (Chapter VII) should be of great value to you.

100

Notes

* There is no one way to play any of these riffs. The idea is to MOLD them to the music, to the beat, to your mood.

* When you make a mistake, DON'T STOP PLAYING. Simply continue blowing and drawing until you get to a Note of Resolution or a Wailing Note. When in doubt, fake it.

* When practicing these blues riffs, keep a steady 1 – 2 – 1 – 2 or 1 – 2 – 3 – 4 beat going with your foot.

* Use TONGUING to add rhythm and tension to Wailing Notes and Notes of Resolution.

* SIMPLICITY and REPETITION are important features of good harp music. For instance, the Good Morning Riff played again and again will usually sound better than the Complete Blues Scale Down or Complete Blues Scale Up.

* Feel free to use the patterns in this chapter as inspiration for making up your own blues patterns.

* Some of the riffs in this chapter are quite difficult. Don't feel you need to be able to play them before reading on.

* A tape cassette lesson teaching you these riffs is available from the Cross Harp Press.

SIX

Three Chords of the Blues: Playing Solo

Say good bye to that ancient cave where you learned your first blues riffs and pucker up to modern day harmonica music. Chapter VI gets you playing solo harp in I-IV-V blues cycles. Quite possibly this is the most important chapter in the book. Enjoy.

Solo Harp

There you are, playing your harmonica all by yourself, playing *solo*. You play the Up Riff. You play the Down Riff. You play the Blues Scale Down. You play the Good Morning Riff. The riffs you've been practicing sound great, but how do you link them together into one cohesive jam?

When you're playing with a guitar or a piano, there doesn't seem to be any problem. That's because these instruments play the chords and chord cycles. All the harp does is accompany.

But when you're playing by yourself, it's more difficult. The question you ask yourself is: which riff do I play now?

There are many approaches to playing solo harp music. You can play riffs to create and resolve tension. An example of this is playing the Up Riff (ending on Wailing Note 4 draw), pausing, and playing the Down Riff (resolving the tension on 3 blow).

You can play to create a rhythmic effect. You can do this by tonguing one note, say 3 blow, to a staccato train rhythm, using the Up Riff to wail on 4 draw, and returning to the rhythmic 3 blow.

You can also play your blues riffs in cycles – specifically I-IV-V cycles. When you play your solo music in a I-IV-V cycle, the I Chord of Resolution establishes home base. The IV Stepping Stone Chord moves the music away from home. The Dominant Wailer V Chord moves the music further still. Returning to the I Chord of Resolution provides a sense of completion of the cycle and can also signify the start of a new cycle.

Here's a simple I-IV-V chord cycle for Cross Harp. It's so short and easy you could call it a mini-cycle. Stomping out a $1 - 2 - 1 - 2$ beat, play this cycle over and over. Give each chord two beats. Add tonguing to give special feeling. Imagine these sounds as a musical wheel and make that wheel roll.

1234	1234	45	1234
Resolution	Stepping	Wailing	Resolution
I	IV	V	I

Single Note Cycles

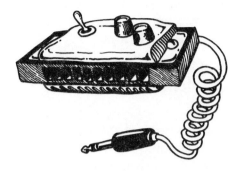

Playing Cross Harp, the single notes that express the I Chord of Resolution are the Notes of Resolution 2 draw, 3 blow, 6 blow and 9 blow.

The notes that express the IV Stepping Stone Chord are Stepping Stone Notes 1 blow, 4 blow, 7 blow and 10 blow.

The single notes expressing the V Dominant Wailer Chord are Wailing Notes 1 draw, 4 draw and 8 draw. Three draw bent down and 6 draw will also work.

Giving each note two beats, play this I-IV-V single note mini-cycle.

3	4	④	3
Resolution	Stepping	Wailing	Resolution
I	IV	V	I

Here's a mini-cycle that has you play the Wailing Note before you play the Stepping Stone Note.

3	④	4	3
Resolution	Wailing	Stepping	Resolution
I	V	IV	I

Try tonguing every note in this mini-cycle twice. Try tonguing in triplets. Tongue as though the harp were having a conversation with itself, making some sounds long and others short. No matter what your tonguing pattern, give each note two steady stomps of your foot. Make that harp go!

Single note progressions can also be played on the low end of your harp. Two draw is the same note as 3 blow. One blow is the same note as 4 blow, but an octave lower. Also one octave down, 1 draw is the same note as 4 draw.

②	1	①	②
Resolution	Stepping	Wailing	Resolution
I	IV	V	I

Tonguing every note of the above progression will get your rhythm going. NOT tonguing the final 2 draw will produce a stronger feeling of resolution. Keep that foot, mouth and breath going as you play progression over and over.

Twelve Bars That Sound So Good

Anyone who listens to the blues has heard the 12 bar blues cycle. It's a long, slow progression with a steady 4 stomp beat. The term "12 bars" refers to 12 sections, each consisting of 4 beats. Playing clear single notes and stomping 1 – 2 – 3 – 4 – 1 – 2 – 3 – 4, play this single note blues cycle again and again. Tonguing each note will help make it more bluesy.

Twelve Bars for Beginner's Cycle

I	Note of Resolution	3	(4 Beats)
IV	Stepping Stone Note	4	(4 Beats)
I	Note of Resolution	3	(4 Beats)
I	Note of Resolution	3	(4 Beats)
IV	Stepping Stone Note	4	(4 Beats)
IV	Stepping Stone Note	4	(4 Beats)
I	Note of Resolution	3	(4 Beats)
I	Note of Resolution	3	(4 Beats)
V	Dominant Wailer Note	④	(4 Beats)
IV	Stepping Stone Note	4	(4 Beats)
I	Note of Resolution	3	(4 Beats)
V	Dominant Wailer	④	(4 Beats)

(Start the cycle again)

106

Riff Cycles

The next stage in playing dynamite solo Cross Harp to the I-IV-V progression is to use riffs that:

1. End on a Note of Resolution to express the I chord.
2. End on Stepping Stone Note 1 blow, 4 blow, 7 blow or 10 blow to express the IV chord.
3. End on Wailing Note 1 draw, 4 draw, 6 draw, 8 draw or 3 draw bent down to express the V chord.

For instance, the Down Riff ends on 3 blow. Use it as a Riff of Resolution.

Down Riff
④ 4 ③ 3

To express the IV chord, play a riff that ends on a Stepping Stone Note, say, 4 blow.

④ ④ ④ 4

Tongue the 4 draw three times, then play 4 blow.

To play a Dominant Wailer V Riff, use Wailing Note 4 draw in the Up Riff.

Up Riff
3 ③ 4 ④

Resolve your blues cycle with the Down Riff, giving the home base 3 blow a feeling of finality and completion.

Down Riff
④ 4 ③ 3

Try playing these riffs so they create a blues cycle.

Beginner's Blues Cycle

I	Riff of Resolution	(4) 4 (3) 3
IV	Stepping Stone Riff	(4)(4)(4) 4
V	Dominant Wailer Riff	3 (3) 4 (4)
I	Riff of Resolution	(4) 4 (3) 3

You can play the Wailing V Riff BEFORE you play the Stepping Stone IV Riff and get another simple blues progression.

Stomp N' Tongue Blues Cycle

I	Riff of Resolution	(4) 4 (3) 3
V	Dominant Wailer Riff	3 (3) 4 (4)
IV	Stepping Stone Riff	(4)(4)(4) 4
I	Riff of Resolution	(4) 4 (3) 3

On the low end of your harp, use 2 draw to end your Riff of Resolution, 1 blow as a Stepping Stone Riff ending, and 4 draw to put the wail in your Wailing Riff.

Good Morning Blues Cycle

I	Riff of Resolution	(1) 2 (2)(2)
IV	Stepping Stone Riff	2 3 2 1
V	Dominant Wailer Riff	(4) 4 (3)(4)
I	Riff of Resolution	(4) 4 (3) 3

Another way to play the I-IV-V cycle is to use 6 blow to end your Riff of Resolution and 6 draw to create the Dominant Wailer Riff.

Blues for Pamina Cycle

I	Riff of Resolution	(6) 6 (5)(4) 4 (3) 3
IV	Stepping Stone Riff	(4)(4)(4) 4
V	Dominant Wailer Riff	(4)(5) 6 (6)
I	Riff of Resolution	(6)(6)(6) 6

More Solo Cycles

Here are some blues cycles that use more than four riffs. Pause between riffs if you want, but keep the beat going.

Prosperity Blues Cycle

I	Riff of Resolution	3 ③ 4 ④ ④ 4 ③ 3
IV	Stepping Stone Riff	④④④ 4
I	Riff of Resolution	④ 4 ③ 3
V	Dominant Wailer	④④④④
IV	Stepping Stone Riff	④④④ 4
I	Riff of Resolution	④ 4 ③ 3
V	Dominant Wailer	3 ③ 4 ④
	or	
I	Riff of Resolution	3 ③③ 3

This blues cycle can be concluded by playing the Riff of Resolution twice. Or, it can be continued by playing the Riff of Resolution once and then playing a Wailing Riff. Playing this Wailing Riff at the end of the blues cycle is called a TURN-AROUND. The turn-around ends the blues cycle in a state of tension on the V chord, and makes you want to play it again.

The first two times you play the above cycle, use the turn-around. The third time you play it, resolve on the Riff of Resolution.

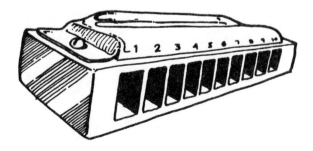

This next blues cycle uses another combination of Wailing Notes and Notes of Resolution.

Jamaica Blues Cycle

I	Riff of Resolution	(6)(6)(6) 6	
V	Dominant Wailer	6 (5)(4)(4)	
IV	Stepping Stone Riff	(4)(5)(4) 4	
I	Riff of Resolution	(1) 2 (2)(2)	
V	Dominant Wailer	3 (3) 4 (4)	
IV	Stepping Stone Riff	(4)(4)(4) 4	
I	Riff of Resolution	(1) 2 (2)(2)	

V	Dominant Wailer	(2)(3) 4 (4)
	or	
I	Riff of Resolution	3 (3)(3) 3

This example of a blues cycle uses the high end of your harp.
Up here, 9 blow is often used as a Note of Resolution. Eight draw is a Wailing Note, and 7 blow is a Stepping Stone Note.

Tia's Blues Cycle

I	Riff of Resolution	(8)(9) 9 9
V	Dominant Wailer	9 (9) 8 (8)
IV	Stepping Stone Riff	(8)(8)(8) 7
I	Riff of Resolution	(6)(6)(6) 6
V	Dominant Wailer	6 (7) 7 (8)
IV	Stepping Stone Riff	(8) 9 (9) 7
I	Riff of Resolution	(6)(6)(6) 6

V	Dominant Wailer	6 (7) 7 (8)
	or	
I	Riff of Resolution	6 (7)(8)(7) 6

110

Twelve Bar Blues for Harp

Here's a 12 bar blues cycle using simple Cross Harp Riffs. Stomping your foot, try to keep each riff within a 4 beat framework.

Ocean Wave Blues Cycle

I	Riff of Resolution	④ 4 ③ 3
IV	Stepping Stone Riff	④④④ 4
I	Riff of Resolution	④ 4 ③ 3
I	Riff of Resolution	④ 4 ③ 3
IV	Stepping Stone Riff	④④④ 4
IV	Stepping Stone Riff	④④④ 4
I	Riff of Resolution	④ 4 ③ 3
I	Riff of Resolution	④ 4 ③ 3
V	Dominant Wailer Riff	3 ③ 4 ④
IV	Stepping Stone Riff	④④④ 4
I	Riff of Resolution	④ 4 ③ 3
V	Dominant Wailer	3 ③ 4 ④

Play this cycle again and again. Tongue your 4 draws and 3 blows to add meaning and feeling. Now that's the blues!

This 12 bar blues cycle concentrates on the low end of your harp. Two draw is sometimes difficult for beginners. Remember to draw lightly, to pull the air stream towards the top of your head and to push your harp and upper lip up towards your nose.

Evening Star Blues Cycle

I	Riff of Resolution	①2②②
IV	Stepping Stone Riff	2 3 2 1
I	Riff of Resolution	①2②②
I	Riff of Resolution	①2②②
IV	Stepping Stone Riff	④④④4
IV	Stepping Stone Riff	④④④4
I	Riff of Resolution	①2②②
I	Riff of Resolution	①2②②
V	Dominant Wailer	3③4④
IV	Stepping Stone Riff	④④④4
I	Riff of Resolution	①2②②
V	Dominant Wailer	①2②③4④

Notes

* The framework of blues, rock, country western, reggae, new wave et. al. is the I-IV-V CHORD PROGRESSION.

* When accompanying a guitar or piano, the harp player lets these instruments play the I-IV-V Chord Progression.

* WHEN PLAYING SOLO, the harp player plays riffs, patterns of notes that express the progression.

* The basic idea is to play riffs that end on a Note of Resolution to express the I chord, riffs that end on a Wailing Note to express the V chord, and riffs that end on Stepping Stone Note 1 blow, 4 blow, 7 blow or 10 blow to express the IV chord.

* The I-IV-V blues cycle is NOT CARVED IN CONCRETE. The order of riffs can be changed and one riff can be substituted for another.

* The only set rule is that the harp player establishes a home base.

* As the harp player plays the cycle, he or she can use 3 blow as a Note of Resolution one time, 6 blow or 9 blow the next time. Similarly, one Wailing Note can be exchanged for another, one Stepping Stone for another.

* Learning the progressions in this chapter will enhance your harp playing; but the way they sound, the tempo at which they're played, their overall feeling is up to you.

* A tape cassette lesson playing these cycles is available from the Cross Harp Press.

SEVEN

The Sensuous Harmonica Player

What's it like to bend notes? To make your harmonica laugh, cry, coo and wail? Here, at last, are the unabridged answers. In explicit language, the author takes you deep into the heart and soul of the harmonica, and helps you develop a meaningful relationship with this very sensuous musical instrument.

115

The Sensuous Instrument

Though rarely described in this way, the harmonica is a sensuous instrument – both in the sounds it makes and in the relationship it has with the person who plays it.

For example, the way a harmonicist plays a single note is similar to a kiss. Lips pucker out to embrace the instrument. Mouth is slightly open. Throat opens itself to the unobstructed passage of air. All movement occurs with gentle firmness and rhythmic sensuality.

Only in the embrace of a sensuous single note can the harmonica communicate the musical feelings the player wants so badly to express. Hands open and close, changing the tone from *ahhhhh* to *oooooo*. Notes bend down and curve upwards to create and resolve tension. Tongue *ta ta ta*'s the fleshy ridge behind the upper teeth. Foot stomps a beat on the floor. Harp slides across moist lips. Riffs tremble out unconsciously as the harp plays the player and the player plays the harp.

Harmonica playing is like dancing. The body responds to its own music. There's no self-criticism, no self-judgment. Though structured in a basic understanding of notes, scales, blows and draws, this dance is freeform and individual. It is a dance of breath, tongue, lips, hands, throat and mouth.

There's no other dance like the one that comes to you naturally. It's your rhythm, your style, your mood. It belongs to you, you and the object of your affections, the harmonica.

Breathing—How to Avoid Passing Out When Playing Harp

Playing Cross Harp, the beginning harp player's lungs are often filled to capacity from drawing so much. Here are some tips to help you deal with this problem.

Consider: if you take a QUICK deep breath, you can fill your lungs in about half a second.

On the other hand, if you take a SLOW deep breath you can keep the air streaming into your lungs for 10, 15, 20 or even 30 seconds.

This slow sucking and blowing of air is the way you should meet your body's breathing needs. Watch the second hand of a clock as you play 4 draw. See how long you can make the note last. When your lungs are almost filled, blow on hole 3. Keep the airstream controlled instead of allowing it to explode into your harp. How long can you make the 3 blow last? When your lungs are almost empty, draw on hole 4 again. Then play a long, controlled blow.

Working with this blow and draw exercise will help you gain control over your breathing. Before long, you'll never run out of breath when playing harmonica.

Some additional tips:

* Excess air in the lungs can be released by playing a blow note, or simply by taking the harp away from your mouth and exhaling.

* Breathing needs can also be satisfied by phrasing your riffs. Play the Up Riff to a 4 stomp beat. Take the harp away from your mouth for 4 stomps. Then play the Down Riff to the same four stomp cadence. Remember, silence is an integral part of music.

* When blowing, don't puff your cheeks. Rather, draw your cheeks *in* a little bit to help guide the airstream down the center of your mouth.

The Sensuous Bender

You are playing the Up Riff. Harp is set well between your puckered lips. Upper lip rests comfortably on the upper plate of the harp. To facilitate this, harmonica is tilted slightly down, into your mouth.

With an up and out pucker, you guide a gentle blow into hole 3. Immediately, the airstream reverses itself to coax 3 draw through the reeds. In almost the same motion, you move the harp to hole 4 and blow. Without the slightest hesitation, you draw.

And there you are, wailing on 4 draw, creating musical tension as the sound of your harmonica fills the room.

A large, vibrant airstream channels through the harp, tickling the insides of your puckered lips and narrowed cheeks, splashing against the back of your throat, cascading down into your voice box and lungs.

Now, you hollow out your throat and draw the airstream directly into your voice box. With an almost mirrored response, the 4 draw swoops down, playing the note much lower than usual.

This flattening of the note creates even more tension as your 4 draw Wailer bounces off the walls. The ear that hears this curving tone is pleased and surprised.

Slowly, you release the air pressure from your voice. As the focus of the airstream moves slowly up your throat, the flattened 4 draw bends slowly upwards.

The ear leans forward. What is happening here?

118

Pounding your foot to a 4 stomp beat, you return to 3 blow – but not to resolve tension. No, it's much too soon for that.

You've come back to the 3 blow to play the Up Riff again. Blow-draw on hole 3, blow-draw on hole 4. As you play this fabulous 4 draw Wailing Note, you suck the air deep into your voice box... and release it.

The 4 draw has now played two notes, 4 draw bent and 4 draw unbent. The way the flattened 4 draw slurred up into the unbent 4 draw has pleased and excited the ear. It isn't exactly sure what happened – but it sure felt good.

What next? Appreciating the importance of repetition in music, you play the Up Riff once again. Only this time when you draw on hole 4, you quickly shift the focus of the airstream from throat to voice box, throat to voice box.

Weee ewe weee ewe weee ewe! Your lips wiggle and your throat and mouth hollow out as though whistling these vowel sounds on the inhale.

Naturally, the harp responds perfectly. The *weeee* vowel sound drawn through hole 4 plays an unbent single note.

The *ewe* sound automatically hollows out the throat and changes the shape of the lips. In this position, the airstream curves down to the voice box, and the 4 draw does exactly what the airstream does. It curves down almost a full note.

Immediately, mouth and throat return to the *weee* position, and the air pressure shoots to the top of your throat. The note curves to the top of its bending range.

Ewe. The note dips down. *Weee.* The note bends up.

Weee ewe weee ewe weee ewe!

Four draw wails like this for four beats.

On the fourth beat, the listening ear is now tingling with anticipation. What will you do now?

You rat! You've built all this tension and you've stopped playing.

You're pausing. That's right. You've stopped playing, but your foot keeps right on stomping. The tension of that long, wailing 4 draw hangs in the air. 1-2-1-2 stomps your foot. 1-2-1-2.

Again, you play a quick bending 4 draw going *wee ewe, wee ewe, wee ewe.* Four beats pass. Then, the 4 draw curves down towards the 4 blow. Your breath reverses as the note hits the low part of the bend. Now, you're playing the 4 blow. Without a pause, you move the harp to hole 3 and draw this molasses-thick note into your voice box. The tension is incredible as the 3 draw bends deeper and deeper. You're almost to the Note of Resolution, 3 blow – but not quite.

The ear quivers, "Oh, give it to me! Give me that Note of Resolution!"

"Do you really want it?" the deeply bent 3 draw asks.

"Oh, yes! More than anything!" cries the ear.

The 3 draw bends lower still. Almost to resolution, but still a hair's breadth away.

"Please! Don't tease me. I can't stand it!" cries the frantic ear.
The air pressure in your hollowed-out voice box travels slightly up, then back down. Gently, you blow.

"Ahhhhh," sighs the ear. "Resolution. It feels soooo good." It staggers, almost falling off the head of its owner. Then it says, "That was incredible. Could you do it again. PLEASE?"

The Practical Bender

Dig it. Bending isn't a talent. It's a knack. The first step of acquiring this knack is getting a clear single note with an out and up pucker and the harp deep in your lips.

Once you're playing full single notes, move the focus of your drawn airstream from the back of your throat DOWN into your voice box. This *manipulation* of your airstream is similar to whistling high and then whistling low – except that the whistle is on the draw instead of the blow.*

When you draw a note into your voice box, you hollow out your throat. This hollowing guides the airstream down to the area where you swallow. It feel somewhat like yawning, except that you keep your lips puckered.

Here are some tips for benders:

* Pucker sensuously when you bend.

* Keep the volume of your note constant.

* When bending, do not drop or clench your jaw. Don't grimace, or tighten up.

* Don't wiggle the tip of your tongue.

* Don't play all your notes bent, or there will be no bend, only flat notes. Play notes in both the bent and unbent positions.

---

* On holes 1 through 6, you can bend only the draw notes. On holes 7 through 10, you can bend blow notes.

Bending One Draw and Four Draw

On your **C** harp:
One draw and 4 draw (same notes but an octave apart) are usually easiest to bend. In regular blues playing, 4 draw is played more than 1 draw.

Some basic bends are:

Two Step Bend

Slur your 4 draw bent to 4 draw unbent.

Wailing Bend

Make the 4 draw undulate between high and low by quickly shifting the focus of air pressure from shallow throat to deep throat.

Tongue Bend

Bend the 4 draw down as you tongue triplets. Keep tonguing as you slowly bring the note back up. The result is a rhythmic staccato of curving notes that perfectly blend into each other.

Tongue Wailer Bend

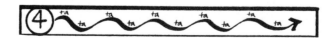

Tongue the high and low spots of the undulating wailing bend. You get a staccato of high, low, high, low, etc.

Fancy Tongue Wailer Bend

Tongue the unbent 4 draw twice and the bent 4 draw once. This is one of an infinite number of variations on the tongue-bend theme.

Some riffs on which to bend or tongue-bend the 4 draw are:

Up Riff
3 ③ 4 ④

Down Riff
④ 4 ③ 3

Six Blow to Four Draw Down
6 ⑤④

Bending Two Draw

As a rule of thumb (or lip), if you are able to get a clear single note on the 2 draw of your **C** harp, you are playing single notes correctly.

On the other hand, if your 2 draw won't respond, your single note technique needs help. Try moving the harp UP towards your nose. Relax your lips, but keep a deep, sensuous pucker. As you draw, direct that airstream to the roof of your mouth. Pull that note UP.

Now, the unbent 2 draw is a Note of Resolution. It's the same note as 3 blow. The advantage of 2 draw is that you can get there quickly from 1 draw and 2 blow – and you can bend 2 draw down an entire note.

The note you bend down to is a Stepping Stone Note. It's essentially the same note as 5 draw, only down an octave. Use this bent 2 draw to create tension and expectation for the unbent 2 draw.

Start by getting a clear single note on 2 draw. Then suck the note down, deep into your voice box. Your 2 draw may distort, but that's okay as long as the note is actually lowering. In fact, a distorted, bent 2 draw is one of the hallmark sounds of blues harp.

When the note pulls down, hold it there. Then gradually allow the bent 2 draw to return to its unbent position.

Two Step Bend

When you are able to bend 2 draw down and back up, try *starting* the bend with the bent 2 draw and slowly bring it up.

Wailing Bend

Try bending 2 draw up and down very quickly. Remember to end the bend on the unbent 2 draw Note of Resolution.

Two Step Tongue Bend

Tongue the note in triplets. The first two syllables should be in the low part of the bend. The third should announce the high part.

The Good Morning Riff is an excellent way to use the bending potential of 2 draw.

Good Morning Riff
① 2 ②

②	RESOLUTION / Stepping
2	Stepping Stone
①	WAILING

Bending Three Draw

To play good blues harp, you need to learn to bend 3 draw just right. There are three possible notes within the 3 draw. The 3 draw unbent is the 3rd note of the 1-3-5 combination of harmonizing notes. Although it will always work when accompanying a I-IV-V chord progression, unbent 3 draw will not sound bluesy. And, if your guitarist is using the seventh chord in his I-IV-V progression, the 3 draw unbent may not work at all.

When you lower the 3 draw by bending, you play the 2½ note of the major scale. This is the blues harmonizing note discovered by Adam.

If you bend the 3 draw even lower, you'll play the 2nd note of the major scale – and this too can sound very bluesy.

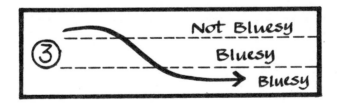

③	Not Bluesy
	Bluesy
	Bluesy

There may be a feeling of resistance in the airstream you draw through hole 3. Somehow this note feels *thicker* than the 4 draw or 6 draw. Once you get used to it, this feeling of thickness can give you amazing control in bending the 3 draw.

Don't force the 3 draw. Coax it. Kiss the harmonica fully and sensuously. Make the airstream large and pull 3 draw down to your guts. Then blow on hole 3. That's the only way to do it.

Establish your Note of Resolution by tonguing the 3 blow. Play 3 draw bent, continuing your tonguing. Then resolve on 3 blow.

Three Draw and Blow Boogie

3 ③ 3

Q means draw and bend down

Bending Six Draw

Six draw is the same note as the bent 3 draw, except it is an octave higher. Since 6 draw is a Wailing Note, you can tongue and bend it through an entire blues cycle. You can easily resolve the tension created by 6 draw by playing Note of Resolution 6 blow.

Six Draw Wail and Six Blow Resolution

Some effective bends on the 6 draw are:

Two Step Bend

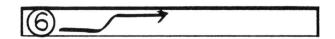

Tongue Bend

wailing Bend

Riffs that work well with the 6 draw bending are:

Upper Riff

3 ③ 4 ④ ⑥ 6

Play the Up Riff. Wail on 4 draw. Without stopping your draw, slide to 6 draw. Wail and bend to create tension. Resolve on 6 blow.

Nine Blow Down

9 ⑨ 8 ⑧ ⑦⑥ 6

Before resolving on the 6 blow, stretch the 6 draw out, slowly curving it towards the Note of Resolution. When you go from 6 draw to 6 blow, reverse your breath smoothly. Make it seem that the 6 draw has slurred down into the 6 blow.

What About Five Draw?

Playing Cross Harp, 5 draw is a Stepping Stone Note. Then why does it sound so good when you play it by mistake? Five draw is the 6½ note of Adam's Blues Scale. It won't harmonize throughout an entire I-IV-V progression, but when you use it as a Stepping Stone, 5 draw is a great note.

Try the 4 and 5 Draw Slide: quickly swivel your harp between holes 4 and 5. Don't stop your single note draw. This 4 and 5 Draw slide adds a warbling blues sound to your music. Use it to create musical tension.

Here's another riff using the 5 draw.

Five Draw Descender
⑤ 5 ④ 5 ④ 4 ③ 3

Experiment with your 5 draw. Don't play it too loud, too long, too often: but play it!

Bending Nine Blow

Yes, Virginia, you *can* bend blow notes. But only the high ones. In particular, the Note of Resolution, 9 blow. The idea is to bend it down to create a sense of tension, and to bend it back up to release the tension.

The first step in bending 9 blow is getting a clear single note. Then you push your airstream forward and DOWN into the harmonica. To bring the bend back up, let the focus of air pressure in the harmonica rise. This is easiest on the lower key harps such as **G** or **A**.

Nine blow can be played in a wailing bend:

It can be curved down to slur into the next lowest note, 9 draw. This is especially effective on a riff that heads down such as the 9 Blow Down.

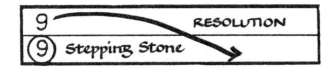

128

Nine blow can also be curved down and up to blend into 10 blow—
a Stepping Stone Note that sounds bluesy when bent.

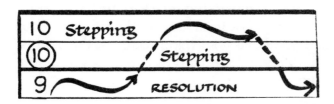

Practice bending your 9 blow in the 6 Blow Up Riff.

Six Blow Up
6 ⑦⑧ ᵇ 9

Your Hands—
How To Make Your Harp Talk

If you want, your harmonica can be a church organ inside a
cathedral. A funky cathedral, true. But would you have it any other
way?

The cathedral is your cupped hands. They create an air chamber
around your harp. With this air chamber open, your harp says
ahhhhhhhh on a note such as 3 blow. When your hands close,
sealing the chamber around the harp, 3 blow says *ooooooooooo*
(pronounced *ewe*).

By going from closed to open on 3 blow three times in a row, you
can make your harp say *oooooo ahhhhhh ooooooo ahhhhhhhh
oooooooo ahhhhhhhhhh*.

Playing 3 blow with your hands closed and quickly opening them
makes the harp say *waaaa*. Doing it twice makes the harp say
waaaa waaaa.

You can use your hands to shape your tones, giving notes a talking
quality. You can also use them to punctuate your music much as

you use tonguing to break a long blow or draw into a chain of staccato pieces.

In addition, you can combine the effects your hands create with tonguing and bending. For instance, bending 4 draw down is enhanced when you keep your hands open at the start of the bend, close them as you bring the note down, and open them as you bring the note back up.

The same is true of any note you bend. Closing your hands makes the note deeper. The sealed air chamber gives added control in bending the note. It mellows your tone, sweetens your sound, and adds a new dimension to your harp playing.

Cupping your hands works best on your low notes – holes 1 through 6. This means your cup doesn't have to provide an air chamber for the entire harmonica. Forming your cup to cover only the lower notes will do quite nicely.

There are two basic styles of cups for harp players. One is for small hands. The other is for large hands.

If you have small hands, place the harp between the thumb and forefinger of your left hand. Form an upside-down cup with four fingers of your left hand.

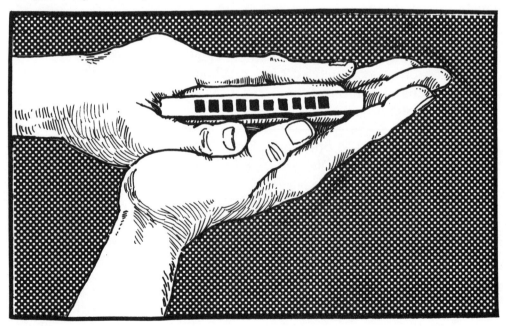

With your right hand, form a cup and place it beneath the harp holding thumb of your left hand. Curve the palm and fingers of your right hand's cup so there is an air chamber beneath the lower four holes of your harp.

To open the cup, swing the right hand down about an inch. Use the connection between the heel of your cupped right hand and your left hand's harp-holding thumb as a hinge. Make this closing and opening motion smooth. You don't have to drop the right hand's palm very far to make the harp say *wa!*

Some additional tips for people using the small hand cupping technique:

* When holding the harp between the thumb and forefinger of your left hand, be sure you're gripping the harp towards the back of the instrument. Otherwise, your fingers will keep you from getting a sensuous pucker for your single note.

* If you can't get a good *waaaa* by closing and opening your hands search for leaks in your cup and rearrange your hands so that the cup is sealed.

* Make the opening and closing movements of your right hand gentle and smooth. This will make your harp playing more graceful. It will also keep you from losing your single note when you move your hands.

* Once you have the basic idea of forming an air chamber, arrange your hands so they feel natural to you.

For people with large hands, there is another cupping technique. Curve your left hand and place it at a 45 degree angle to the floor. Hold the harmonica by sticking its end in the fleshy notch between the heel of your left hand and the thumb. DO NOT use your little finger to help balance the harp.

Cup your right hand and place it over your harp-holding left hand. Help balance the harp by placing it against the first inside knuckle of your right hand.

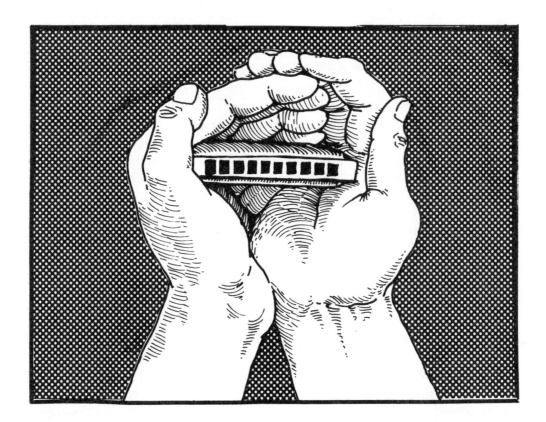

Bring the entire harp and hand apparatus to your puckered lips.
Seal the air chamber beneath the harp by placing the heels of your
hands against both sides of your jaw.

Your right hand can curve around so it practically covers holes
7, 8, 9, 10. When you want to play these holes, pull the hand back
and slide the harp.

As with the small hand method of cupping the harp, the air chamber
is beneath the harmonica. To open the chamber and make your
harp say *wa!*, let your right thumb serve as a hinge for the cupped
right hand. Open the hand and close it. Make the motion smooth,
like dancing.

If your harp's tone isn't responding, look for air leaks. Have you
form-fitted the edges of the heels of your hand to your jaw and chin?
Are your hands relaxed? Have you created an actual pocket out of
your palms and fingers?

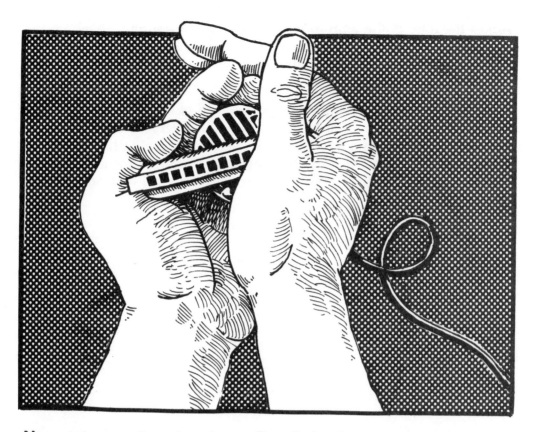

Now, get yourself a microphone. Specific kinds are mentioned in Chapter XI. Cup your hands around that mike and your harp. Plug the mike into an amplifier. YOWWWWW! What was that awful screech? It's called feedback. It's what happens when the sound coming out of your amp is picked up by your microphone.

Step away from your amp so the speaker isn't pointed directly at your microphone. Now, blow and draw. Keep your hands airtight. If you have difficulty cupping the mike and harp at the same time, wrap a piece of wetsuit material (also known as neoprene) around the mike to form a tunnel. A rubber band wrapped around the neoprene will make this semi-permanent.

Now cup the harp to the neoprene tunnel. You should have a perfect air chamber leading directly into your microphrone. The flex-ibility of the neoprene will feel great on your fingers.

Adjust the tone of the amp to accentuate the low sounds. Give yourself lots of volume. Sounds great, but can you turn it up a little? They can't hear you down the street.

With the help of these instructions, find a way of holding and cupping the harmonica that feels good to you. Everyone's hands are a little different, and it follows that everyone cups the harmonica a little bit differently. Think of your hands as dancers, sensuous creatures who love music. Trust them to find a way of making that harp talk.

Notes

* The most important skill in harp playing is being able to get a clear, rich SINGLE note.

* To keep from running out of breath when playing harp, learn the trick of the SLOW INHALE.

* BENDING is a technique in which the harp player lowers the note by manipulating the airstream, pulling it DOWN into the lungs.

* Bending is very difficult if you don't have a good single note with an up and out pucker of your lips. It's not difficult when your single note technique is correct.

* Bending helps the harp player create tension. Below hole 6, bend 1 draw, 2 draw, 3 draw, 4 draw and 6 draw. Above hole 6, bend 8 draw, 9 blow and 10 blow.

* Bending can be combined with TONGUING.

* CUPPING your hands around the harp mellows tone and makes the harp say *ooooooo*. Opening your hands makes the harp say *ahhhhhhhh*.

* Use the instructions on hands to find the way of cupping the harp that feels best to you. Everybody's hands are different, and each harp player's cup is a little different.

EIGHT

Stone Goes Straight

Straight Harp is the style of harmonica that sounds best with ballads and jazz. More melodic than Cross Harp, it's also easier to play. In Chapter VIII, Stone goes straight, brings a woman vocalist to practice and the band tunes up.

The Mysterious Visitor

One Sunday afternoon Stone showed up for practice in a suit and tie.

"Hey!" demanded Smash. "What's going on here?"

Before Stone could answer, a woman stepped into the entrance of the cave. She was tall, slender, and most important to the chauvinist Cave Boys, good-looking.

"Guys," said Stone, "I'd like you to meet a friend of mine. This is Umm."

Six Cave Boy eyes went from Stone to Umm and back to Stone. True, Umm was a dish. But what was this "friend" stuff? If you wanted a woman, you grabbed her by the hair and dragged her back to the cave. You didn't call her "friend." And you sure didn't start wearing a suit and tie.

"Well, do come in," said Krok, nervously fingering his guitar.

"Would you like something to drink?" stammered Smash. "Iced tea maybe?"

Behind her rose-tinted monogrammed "U" glasses, Umm's eyes smiled. The way her hair frizzed out, it looked as though grabbing this lady for a one-night cave encounter would only produce a handful of hairspray.

Umm placed a cigarette in the end of a long, mammoth tusk cigarette holder and lit up. "No thanks," she said to Smash.

"Umm came to hear us play," said Stone.

"I can dig that," said Smash, "But what's with the suit and tie?"

"Listen man," said Stone, "It takes more than grime and sweat to make good music. Let's add a little class to the act. Besides, Umm here has got us a gig."

138

"A gig?" said Krok, "Where?"

Not exactly a gig – an audition," said Umm.
"What's an addition?" asked Smash.
"It's a gig..." offered Stone.
"But you don't get paid," added Gref.
"If they like you, they ask you to come back," said Krok.
"Then they pay you," chimed Stone.

Smash frowned and rubbed his stubby chin. His drumsticks looked like twigs in his huge hands.

"Where is this audition?" asked Krok.

"At The Club," said Umm, "I know the guy who runs the place."

"Let's practice," Stone said. He loosened his necktie. "I gotta new harp style I want to try. If we're gonna audition, we want to be ready. And look..." he turned to Krok, "this time let's tune up before we play."

"Tune up again?" asked Krok with a shudder. He usually tuned the deer sinew guitar strings about every six months. "What the devil for?"

"So it sounds like we're playing in the same key!" shouted Stone. So an **E** note on your guitar and Gref's bass is the same as an **E** note on my harmonica. So the music doesn't sound like a bunch of Neanderthals banging on pots and pans!"

Krok looked carefully at Stone standing there with his hands on his hips; his suit, loosened tie and "friend" giving him a new air of authority.

Tune up? he thought. It had never made any difference before. It was obvious Stone was just trying to impress this frizz-haired Umm sitting over there in a cloud of cigarette smoke. As leader, songwriter and guitarist for the Cave Boys, Krok considered telling Stone to start walking.

But he stopped himself. Good harp players were hard to find. Besides, if he got rid of Stone, he might lose his audition.

"Okay," he finally said to Stone, "Give me a note."

Tuning Guitars
To Harmonicas

On those rare occasions when they did tune, the band always matched notes with Stone's harmonica. It was the only instrument around that didn't change pitch. Bass and guitar strings (especially guitar) got out of tune just sitting around. Hot weather made the strings stretch and get lower. Cold weather made them tighten and get higher.

But when it came to being on key, Stone's harmonica was Old Faithful.

Now, being in tune meant that a certain note on one instrument was the same note on another instrument. The procedure was for Stone to play a note on his harp and for Gref and Krok to tune their instruments to that note.

The guitar strings were set up like this. The first string was tuned to an **E** note. The second one to a **B**, the third to a **G**, the fourth to a **D**, the fifth to an **A**, and the sixth string to an **E**.

Here's how the guitar looked:

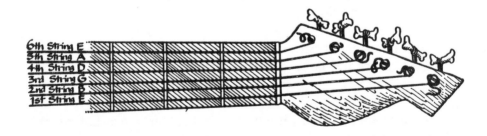

And the bass, a four-stringed instrument, was set up like Krok's guitar. The only difference was that the strings were much thicker and were set down an octave from the guitar.

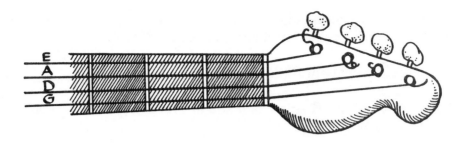

So, on both bass and guitar, the lowest string needed to be tuned to an **E** note. Stone pulled out his **C** harp. The layout of notes looked like this:

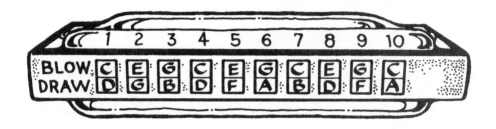

"Gimme an **E**, a low **E**," said Gref.

Stone played a 2 blow on his **C** harp. Bass and guitar strings varoomed as the **E** strings were tightened to play the same note as an **E** on Stone's harmonica.

"Okay, gimme an **A**," said Krok, once his **E** string was in tune.

Stone played a 6 draw, careful not to bend it so Krok and Gref would not be tuning to a flattened note.

Again, bass and guitar strings twanged.

Smash sighed impatiently. Tuning was necessary, he guessed. But it took so long! Why couldn't the band just play and pretend they were in tune?

"How 'bout a **D**?" asked Gref once the **E** and **A** strings on the guitar and bass were the same pitch as the **E** and **A** notes on the harp.

Again careful not to bend the note or cup the harp in his hands, Stone now played a 4 draw on his **C** harp. This was his **D** note.

For the **G** strings, Stone played a 3 blow. Gref was now tuned. His bass had only four strings. But Krok needed a **B** note.

Stone played an unbent 3 draw.

"Varooom!" went the **B** string as it sought out the pitch that would match Stone's **B**.

And for the final note, another **E**, Stone played a higher **E** on his harp: the 5 blow.

Krok carefully tightened the tuning peg and his high **E** string slid up towards the same pitch as the harp's **E** note.

Finally, the two sounds were the same.

Krok strummed a **C** chord. Gref played a riff on the 1-3-5 harmonizing notes of the **C** scale. Stone played a **C** note, the 4 blow on his **C** harp. Even though he didn't need to tune, Smash banged his drums.

"Guess we're there," said Krok.

"Your **B** string is a little flat," said Umm.

"My what?" Krok could not believe he was hearing this.

"Your **B** string," said Umm, smiling sweetly from her cloud of smoke. "Go ahead, strum your **C** chord again. You'll hear it."

Krok strummed each string on his **C** chord. Sure enough, the **B** did sound slightly out of whack. He tightened the tuning peg.

'Mmmmmmmmmmmmm," he said to Umm. "Not only pretty, but smart, too."

"Why don't you guys play something?" she quietly asked.

"Yeah..." said Smash. He brought his sticks down on his snare drums with a tremendous bang.

Stone Jams Straight Harp

"Okay," said Krok, "Let's try that slow love song, 'Cave Angel.' It would go over real good at The Club. Key of **C**. Slow tempo. Guess you'll count up four steps from the **C** and play Cross Harp on an **F** harmonica," he said to Stone.

Stone smiled quietly. "No, I'm gonna do something different on this song. I'm gonna play my **C** harp in the key of **C**. You know... Straight Harp. It sounds more...more..."

"Romantic..." said Umm.

"Yeah, romantic."

Krok squinted at his harp player. Romantic? What had this woman done to him?

"Okay. Here goes," he finally said, "One, two, one, two, three, four..."

Krok strummed the I chord of "Cave Angel." This was, of course, a **C** chord. Gref added supporting notes on his bass, and Smash played a soft steady rhythm.

Then Krok played an **A** minor chord, the relative minor of the **C** chord. From here the music went into an **F** chord, the IV chord of the progression, then it moved to a **G**, the V chord, and returned to the **C**, the I Chord of Resolution.

Using the relative minor chord, the chord 6 steps up the scale from I chord, gave the music a more melodic feeling than did the simple I-IV-V progression. Now the progression went I-VI-IV-V. Although this occurred thousands of years ago, Krok's music sounded remarkably like one of those slow-dance pop ballads that were so popular in the late 1950's and early 60's.

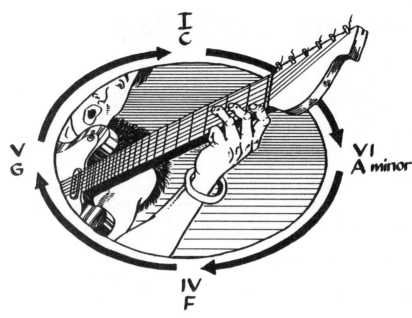

Krok began to sing:

<pre>
C   Am   F   G
"Cave angel, what can I do?
C   Am   F   G
To earn your love so true?
C   Am   F   G   C
Cave angel, will you be mine?"
</pre>

Umm leaned forward. These guys might look rowdy, but they weren't half bad. The blood began to flow more quickly through her heart.

Meanwhile, Stone was preparing to enter the music. He held his **C** harp to his puckered lips.

He hadn't played Straight Harp with the band before. Normally, he used this harp style for playing melodies around a campfire. He couldn't get down and boogie playing Straight Harp. He couldn't get that bluesy, tension-creating feeling.

Still, on this slow moving, pretty love song, bluesy Cross Harp would be out of place. So Straight Harp it was.

144

Straight Harp Revisited

This is the way Straight Harp works (from a Cave Boy's point of view). Take your **C** harmonica and blow on holes 1234. This is your Straight Harp Blow Chord.

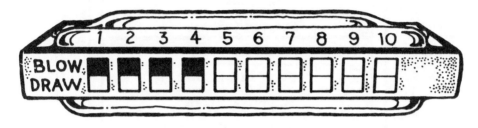

You can also play the Straight Harp Blow Chord by playing holes 4567 blow or 789 and 10 blow. ALL your blow notes are harmonizing notes.

The Notes of Resolution are 1 blow, 4 blow, 7 blow and 10 blow.

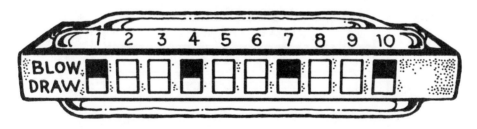

The basic approach, then, to playing improvisational Straight Harp is to accent the blow notes, use the draw notes as Stepping Stones (almost the exact opposite of Cross Harp) and to resolve on 1 blow, 4 blow, 7 blow or 10 blow.

Map of Straight Harp

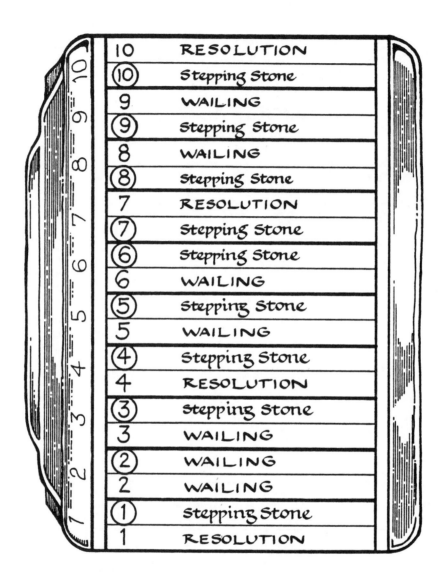

10	RESOLUTION
(10)	Stepping Stone
9	WAILING
(9)	Stepping Stone
8	WAILING
(8)	Stepping Stone
7	RESOLUTION
(7)	Stepping Stone
(6)	Stepping Stone
6	WAILING
(5)	Stepping Stone
5	WAILING
(4)	Stepping Stone
4	RESOLUTION
(3)	Stepping Stone
3	WAILING
(2)	WAILING
2	WAILING
(1)	Stepping Stone
1	RESOLUTION

THE STRAIGHT HARP I CHORD OF RESOLUTION is expressed with single notes 1 blow, 4 blow, 7 blow and 10 blow.

THE IV STEPPING STONE CHORD is expressed with single notes 5 draw, 9 draw and 2 draw bent down.

THE DOMINANT WAILER V CHORD is expressed with single notes 2 draw, 3 blow, 6 blow and 9 blow.

146

As you play Straight Harp, you'll discover that the draw notes – although they're called Stepping Stone Notes – *almost* harmonize. Stepping Stone Notes like 1 draw, 4 draw and 6 draw can be drawn out, accented, as long as a Note of Resolution follows them, or as long as the song isn't on the I chord of the I-IV-V progression.

So, if you're getting clear, single notes, it's pretty hard to make a mistake playing Straight Harp.

Here's a simple Straight Harp Riff that will always harmonize if you are in tune with the guitarist and are playing the right key of harmonica.

Meadow Lark Melody Run
5 ④ 4

You can also play the Meadow Lark Melody Run on the high and low end of your harmonica.

High Meadow Lark Melody Run
8 ⑧ 7

Low Meadow Lark Melody Run
2 ① 1

You can play an Up and Down Meadow Lark Melody Run by returning to the Straight Harp Wailing Note 5 blow immediately after playing the 4 blow.

Up and Down
Meadow Lark Melody Run
5 ④ 4 5 5 ④ 4

High Up and Down
Meadow Lark Melody Run
8 ⑧ 7 8 8 ⑧ 7

147

As mentioned earlier, Straight Harp does not create a bluesy wailing tension in the manner of Cross Harp. And, beneath 7 blow, the blow notes can't be bent.

However, on hole 7 and above, the blow notes *can* be bent. By pushing the airstream forward and down, you can make your 7 blow, 8 blow, 9 blow and 10 blow swoop down. And, by releasing the air you've directed down into your harmonica, you can bring these Straight Harp Harmonizing Notes back to the top of their bending potentials.

For instance, you can create tension on the High Meadow Lark Melody Run by bending the 8 blow Wailing Note.

And, you can resolve the tension with the Straight Harp Descender, a pattern that takes you from Straight Harp Wailing Note 8 blow down to Straight Harp Note of Resolution 4 blow.

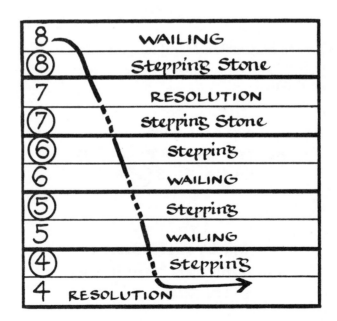

Straight Harp Descender
8 ⑧ 7 ⑥ 6 5 4

8	WAILING
⑧	Stepping Stone
7	RESOLUTION
⑦	Stepping Stone
⑥	Stepping
6	WAILING
⑤	Stepping
5	WAILING
④	Stepping
4	RESOLUTION

From the 4 blow, you can wind your way to the Wailing Note 8 blow.

Straight Harp Ascender
4 ④ 5 6 7 ⑧ 8

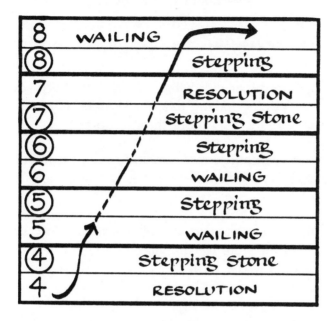

8	WAILING
⑧	stepping
7	RESOLUTION
⑦	stepping stone
⑥	stepping
6	WAILING
⑤	stepping
5	WAILING
④	stepping stone
4	RESOLUTION

These patterns should give you a few ideas for Straight Harp improvisational accompaniment. You can use them as "fillers" – musical phrases that keep a song interesting, or you can use them to create solos. Built on a framework of Straight Harp Harmonizing Notes, the mood and timing of these riffs can be modified to fit the song you're accompanying.

In addition, you can figure out almost all melodies that use a major scale and play them in the Straight Harp Style. The only major scale on your diatonic harp starts on 4 blow and goes:

4 ④ 5 ⑤ 6 ⑥ ⑦ 7
do re mi fa so la ti do

So if your band were going to release a new version of "Old Mac-Donald Had A Farm," you, the harp player, could toot around on this major scale until you discovered the melody.

7   7   7   6   ⑥ ⑥ 6
Old MacDonald had a farm
8   8   ⑧   ⑧   7
Eeeeeyyyy eeeeeyyyy ohhhh

But say the record producer didn't like the way the harp sounded. "C'mon," he says, "You're making this MacDonald guy sound like a pansy. How 'bout some lower, more throaty notes?"

Then you might go searching for the melody on your lower notes – and to your dismay, you'd discover there isn't a complete scale from 1 blow to 4 blow.

You'd find that the *fa* was missing as well as the *la*. You would NOT be able to play the note for the word "had" in those poignant lines, "Old MacDonald had a farm."

4   4   3   ?   3
Old Mac Donald had a farm

Panic sets in! Here you are on the verge of a big recording contract – and you can't find the note for "had."

What you need is a major scale from 1 blow to 4 blow. Okay. Here's what you do. There are notes missing between 2 blow and 2 draw and between 3 blow and 3 draw.

The only way to play a major scale is to bend to 2 draw down before playing the unbent 2 draw, and to bend the 3 draw down before playing the unbent 3 draw.

1   ① 2 ② ② ③ ③ 4
do re mi fa so la ti do

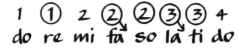 means draw and bend down

150

The note you'd need for playing the "had" in "Old MacDonald" would
be the 3 draw bent down.

```
   4    4    3      ③      3
 Old MacDonald  had a farm
   5    5       ④   ④    4
 Eeeeeyyyy eeeeyyyy ohhh
```

"Perfect!" cries the producer. "You're going to go a long ways with
this little tune!"

So, to enhance your ability in playing Straight Harp melodies,
practice this major scale starting from 1 blow.

```
  1   ①   2  ②   ②  ③③  4
 do  re  mi  fa  so  la  ti  do
```

And also learn to play the major scale going from 4 blow to 1 blow.

```
  4   ③   ③   ②   ②   2  ①  1
 do  ti  la  so  fa  mi  re  do
```

This may be the most difficult technique in the entire book. Still,
when "Old MacDonald" strikes it big and your group has started a
whole new musical genre, "Punk Nursery Rhymes," don't forget
where you learned it.

~~~

But let's get back to Stone, standing there in the musty cave,
sweating like Niagara in his suit and loosened tie, **C** harp to his lips as
the Cave Boys enter another cycle of this old *be bop* chord progression.

Stone tongues his 4 blow. He slides the harp to 5 blow and plays the
Meadow Lark Melody Run: 5 blow, 4 draw, 4 blow. He wails on the
8 blow, slips up to the 9 blow and wails there. Back to the 8 blow,
bending the note and releasing it. Then the 8 Blow Descender – 8
blow, 8 draw, 7 blow, 6 draw, 6 blow, 5 blow, 4 blow – hitting that

151

Straight Harp Note of Resolution at exactly the moment the chord progression has gone full cycle and resolves on the I chord.

It sounds so good, Krok almost drops his guitar. His monkey suited harpist has created a spell with his sensitive Straight Harp. Krok closes his eyes and begins to sing.

"I'd take a bath, I'd comb my hair." A soft 8 blow reverberates off the cave walls. "To show you how much I care." The 8 blow curves down and seems to fall through space as Stone plays the 8 Draw Descender. "Cave angel, will you be mine?" The harmonica echoes the voice with the Meadow Lark Melody run. *Wa wa wa!* the 4 blow actually cries.

"Cave angel...." *Wa wa wa*
"Cave angel...." *Wa wa wa*
"Cave angel...." *Wa wa wa*
"Cave angel...." Only this time the voice doesn't belong to Krok. No, Krok's voice is halfway between a belch and a grunt. This voice is rich, expressive. It belongs to Umm. She's standing up, hands clenched to her bosom, eyes closed, mouth open.

"Cave angel, will you be mine?"

The entire cave seems to be swinging back and forth to this sad, gut wrenching melody. Umm's voice is like a musical instrument. The harp punctuates the music, underscores the emotion. Smash keeps a steady beat. Gref's bass is supportive, sensitive.

Finally, the song ends. The musicians are exhausted, but amazed. This girl can sing! Smash is the first to speak.

"Wow! A chick singer!"

Umm glares, "A woman vocalist."

"Well, guys?" Stone asks, "Can she join our band?"

"We couldn't call ourselves the Cave Boys," says Gref.

"Yeah," says Smash, "It would seem funny."

152

Umm looks at the four musicians. These guys weren't bad. And they were nice enough. Dumb, true. But at least they got into the music. Should she? Well, why not?

"I've got an idea," she says, "How 'bout Umm and the Cave Boys?"

"Sounds good to me," grins Stone.

"I like it," says Gref. "What do you think, Krok?"

All eyes turn to guitarist, songwriter and lead singer of the band. "Well, what do you think?"

No answer. But in Krok's mind, the possibilities are spinning like peaches and cherries on a slot machine. First, they get the job at The Club. Then they move on, playing Dinosaur Breath a couple of nights a week (it's a nice little dive near the tar pits), and then maybe to the big time. Money, booze, women…and maybe, just maybe, Umm, too.

He eyes the frizzy-haired phenomenon standing across the cave. Firelight flickers in her hair, sparkles in her "U" monogrammed glasses, throws shadows on her high, delicate cheekbones.

"Well, tell me this," he says, "How are you at singing rock and blues?"

With that Umm opens her mouth and shouts-sings-laughs-cries, "Baby, why you treat me like you do? Whyyyy? Whyyyy? Whyyyy?"

"Oh yeah!" grunts the voice in Krok's head. "Oh yeah!"

He can see it now. Las Vegas. New York. Los Angeles. World tours. Cosmic tours. Records. Royalties. Revenge on all the people who said he'd never make it. And all because of Umm, this sweet little chick singer, Umm.

"Well," he finally says, "Your voice needs work, but I'll spend some extra time working with you."

"Whooopppppeeeeeee!" shouts Smash.

And that is how Stone's Straight Harp added diversity and class to a ragged old band that never would have made it out of the cave.

"Incidentally," said Umm, "I think your **B** string is still a little flat."

Notes

* Two instruments that aren't tuned to each other sound lousy when played at the same time.

* Being IN TUNE means that an **E** note on the guitar is the same as an **E** note on a harp. Ditto for **A, D, G, B** or any other note.

* The guitar tunes to the harmonica. The harp player gives the guitarist a note and tells him or her what note it is. On an **E** harp, 1 blow is an **E**. On a **D** harp, 1 blow is a **D**. On a **G** harp, 1 blow is a **G**.

* On your **C** harmonica, 2 blow and 5 blow are **E** notes. Use the major scale chart on page 141 to figure out where other important guitar tuning notes are located.

* To play the Straight Harp style of harmonica, play a **C** harp in the key of **C**, a **G** harp in the key of **G**, a **D** harp in the key of **D**. Accent the blow notes. Use draw notes as Stepping Stones.

* Playing Straight Harp, the Notes of Resolution are 1 blow, 4 blow, 7 blow and 10 blow.

NINE

Campfire Melodies

Umm, Stone, Krok, Gref and Smash vacation in the mountains and Stone plays a number of songs that sound best when the stars are twinkling and the campfire is burning.

A Circle of Friends

The vacationing band sat around the campfire. The descent of the sun had turned the horizon from blue to purple, and the first stars of the evening were taking a bow in a theatre of clear skies.

Krok threw a log on the fire and a shower of sparks made everyone move. Umm told a joke about smoke keeping away the mosquitos. The laughter and talk drifted into a contented silence. Only the fire seemed lively, snapping and crackling, drawing all eyes into a kaleidoscope of blue and orange warmth.

As the sky darkened, Stone and his friends leaned closer to the glowing logs. The harp man took his harmonica from his pocket and started to softly play.

"Wa wa wa waaaaaa!"

His simple Cross Harp riffs kept beat to the crackling of flame and wood. A jug of wine made its way around the fire, passed hand to hand, hand to mouth.

"Wa wa wa waaaaaa!" sang the harp.
"Wa wa oooooo ahhhh!"

Krok placed some dry wood on the fire and Stone's harmonica energy rose with the flame. So did the energy of his circle of friends. Smash grunted "Amen" after a particularly soulful phrase. "Yeah!" said Gref.

The party had started. The fire danced to the singing harmonica, cracking and popping a fiesty percussion; castanets on fingers of flame. The wine made its sloshing way around the fire once more. Stone brought his music to a close.

"Alright!" said a shadowy face across the fire. It was Umm. "Play some more," she urged. "Play something we can all sing."

"Yeah!" said Smash, carried away by the beauty of the moment. "Play, uh...'Tom Dooley.' You know, that ol' cowboy song. Everybody knows it."

"Play 'I Been Working On The Railroad,'" said Gref.

"Play 'Froggie Went A' Courtin'" giggled Umm.

"Well, okay," said Stone, "but only if you'll sing along."

Shyly, at first, Stone started to play. The cracked voices of Gref and Smash were matched by Umm's higher harmony. Even Krok, who was often embarrassed by innocence and fun, began singing along in his rough-hewn blues voice. Then he even grabbed his backpacking guitar and began strumming chords.

To tell the truth, it didn't sound that great – not for the best rock and blues band in the prehistoric world. But what the hell, they were on vacation, and having a good time.

And, as Umm said, "There's more to life than the blues."

Now, as the fire dances and the band sings alone, you should try a few of the following campfire melodies. The songs are presented to help you learn more about the harmonica, and add to your own campfire repertoire.

Skip To My Lou Straight Harp

5 4 5 6

Skip, skip, skip to my Lou

④ ③ ④ ⑤

Skip, skip, skip to my Lou

5 4 5 6

Skip, skip, skip to my Lou

④ 5 ⑤ 5 ④ 4

Skip to my Lou, my darlin'

Skip To My Lou Straight Harp High End

8 7 8 9

Skip, skip, skip to my Lou

⑧ ⑦ ⑧ ⑨

Skip, skip, skip to my Lou

8 7 8 9

Skip, skip, skip to my Lou

⑧ 8 ⑨ 8 ⑧ 7

Skip to my Lou, my darlin'

Tom Dooley

Cross Harp

①   2 ② ③
Hang down your head Tom Dooley
①   2 ② ③↘
Hang down your head and cry
①   2 ② ③↘
Hang down your head Tom Dooley
③↘   3 2 3
Poor boy you're going to die

Tom Dooley

Straight Harp

6   ⑥ 7 8
Hang down your head Tom Dooley
6   ⑥ 7 ⑧
Hang down your head and cry
6   ⑥ 7 ⑧
Hang down your head Tom Dooley
⑧   7 ⑥7
Poor boy you're going to die

Froggie Went A'Courtin' Cross Harp

3   ③ 3 2 ①② 2 ②
Froggie went a'courtin' and he did ride ahum ahum

③   ④   5 ④ ③ ④   ④
Froggie went a'courtin' and he did ride ahum ahum

③ ④   5 ④ ③
Froggie went a'courtin' and he did ride

3   ③ 3 2 ①② 2 ②
Sword and pistol by his side ahum ahum

Froggie Went A'Courtin' Straight Harp

7   8 7 ⑥ 6 7 ⑥ 7
Froggie went a'courtin' and he did ride ahum ahum

8   9   ⑩ 9 8 9   9
Froggie went a'courtin' and he did ride ahum ahum

8 9   ⑩ 9 8
Froggie went a'courtin' and he did ride

7   8 7 ⑥ 6 7 ⑥ 7
Sword and pistol by his side ahum ahum

Streets Of Laredo   Cross Harp

①②   ③↘   ③   ③3②①
As I walked out in the streets of Lardeo

①②   ③↘   ③③↘ 3 ③↘
As I walked out in Laredo one day

④   4 ③   4 ③ ③↘③   ③↘ 3 ②①
I spied a young cowboy all wrapped in white linen

① ②   ③↘③ ③↘③ 4   ③ ② ③↘ 3
All wrapped in white linen, and as cold as the clay

Streets Of Laredo   Straight Harp

3 4   ④   5   ④4③ 3
As I walked out in the streets of Lardeo

3 4   ④   5④ 4 ④
As I walked out in Laredo one day

6   ⑤ 5 ⑤ 5 ④ 5   ④ 4 ③ 3
I spied a young cowboy all wrapped in white linen

3   4   ④ 5 ④5 ⑤   5 4④ 4
All wrapped in white linen, and as cold as the clay

163

She'll Be Coming 'Round the Mountain Cross Harp

① 2 ②   2 ①   2 ②
She'll be coming 'round the mountain when she comes

2 ③③   ④ ③ ③↘ 3 ③↘
She'll be coming 'round the mountain when she comes

④ 4 ③   ③↘ 3
She'll be coming 'round the mountain

3   2   ③↘ 3
She'll be coming 'round the mountain

①   ③ ③↘ 3 ②↘ ②
She'll be coming 'round the mountain when she comes

She'll Be Coming 'Round the Mountain Straight Harp

6 ⑥ 7   ⑥ 6 5 6 7
She'll be coming 'round the mountain when she comes

7 ⑧ 8   9 8 ⑧ 7 ⑧
She'll be coming 'round the mountain when she comes

9 ⑨ 8   ⑧ 7
She'll be coming 'round the mountain

7   ⑥   ⑧ 7
She'll be coming 'round the mountain

6   8 ⑧ 7 ⑦ 7
She'll be coming 'round the mountain when she comes

164

Pop Goes The Weasel   Cross Harp

②   ③   ③④③   ②
All around the cobbler's bench

①   ②   ③↘   ③   ②
The monkey chased the weasel

①   ②   ③↘   ③④③②
The monkey thought was all in fun

5   ③↘   4   ③   ③
Pop! goes the weasel

Pop Goes The Weasel   Straight Harp

4   ④   5 6 5 4
All around the cobbler's bench

3   4   ④   5 4
The monkey chased the weasel

3   4   ④   5 65 4
The monkey thought was all in fun

⑥   ④   ⑤   5 4
Pop! goes the weasel

Pop Goes The Weasel Straight Harp High End

7 (8)   8 9 8 7

All around the cobbler's bench

6 7   (8)   8 7

The monkey chased the weasel

6 7   (8)   8 9 8 7

The monkey thought was all in fun

(10) (8) (9) 8 7

Pop! goes the weasel

Ol' Grey Mare   Straight Harp High End

6 7   (8) 8   (8) 8 (8) 7

The ol' grey mare, she ain't what she used to be

(8)   7 (8) 7 (6) 8   (8) 8 (8) 7

Ain't what she used to be, ain't what she used to be

6 7   (8) 8   (8) 8 (8) 7

The ol' grey mare, she ain't what she used to be

(8)   8 (8) 7

Many long years ago

166

Ol' Grey Mare

Cross Harp

① ②   ③↓ ③   ③↓ ③ ③↓ 3

The ol' grey mare, she ain't what she used to be

③↓   3 ③↓ 3 ②↓ ③   ③↓ ③ ③↓ 3

Ain't what she used to be, ain't what she used to be

① ②   ③↓ ③   ③↓ ③ ③↓ 3

The ol' grey mare, she ain't what she used to be

③↓   ③ ③↓ 3

Many long years ago

Ol' Grey Mare

Straight Harp

3 4   ④ 5   ④ 5 ④ 4

The ol' grey mare, she ain't what she used to be

④   4 ④ 4 ③ 5   ④ 5 ④ 4

Ain't what she used to be, ain't what she used to be

3 4   ④ 5   ④ 5 ④ 4

The ol' grey mare, she ain't what she used to be

④   5 ④ 4

Many long years ago

167

TEN

Third Position Slant Harp A Big Time Harp Style

Slant Harp is the style of harmonica many harpists use to accompany songs in Minor Keys. Most appropriate for blues and rock, Slant Harp uses 4 draw as a Note of Resolution.

In Chapter X, Stone makes a television appearance, discovers the secrets of Slant Harp, and finally understands the purpose of musical artistry.

Stone Looks For
A New Harp Style

"There has to be a way. There has to be..." Stone was walking down the mountainside, muttering to himself. His feet slipped on the trailside rocks, and once he even ran into a tree, but the harp-playing Cave Boy barely noticed his own clumsiness. He was bummed.

This had never happened to Stone before. He had ALWAYS been able to provide great accompaniment to any song Umm and the Cave Boys played.

But Krok's new tune, a reggae-flavored ditty called "Volcano Mouth," was giving him trouble. The song was in the key of **A** minor, and for some reason, neither Cross nor Straight Harp sounded very good.

Making matters worse, today was the day of the television appearance. The Cave Boys were scheduled to play on the Dinah Sledgehammer Show, and Krok wanted to introduce "Volcano Mouth" to the fans.

"Listen," he had said to Stone. "If you can't figure out what to play, then don't. No harmonica sounds better than lousy harmonica." Krok had put his arm protectively around Umm's shoulder. "Besides, you wouldn't want to do anything to harm Umm's career, would you?"

"Oh, c'mon," Umm had said, wriggling away from Krok. "It doesn't sound *that bad*."

Doesn't sound that bad, Stone had repeated to himself. *Doesn't sound that bad*. The purpose of his playing was to sound great. No one had ever said *doesn't sound that bad* about his harp-playing before.

"Hey!" he had sputtered, "I'll figure out something. Ol' Harp Boy Stone can play anything." His nervous laugh had been cut off by Krok's abrupt remark. "Why not just bang a tambourine? We've got harmonica on too many songs already."

Now, walking down the mountain trail to the theatre where the show was to be held, Stone brooded over his problem. Playing songs in minor keys had never troubled him before. A minor chord was only a slight variation of a major chord.

Instead of playing the 1st, 3rd and 5th notes of a major scale to form a major chord, what Krok did was strum the 1st, 2½nd and 5th notes of the major scale. This resulted in a minor chord.

To accompany, Stone would ask what key the song was in. If Krok answered, "**A** minor," Stone would count four steps up the scale from **A** (including the **A**)...

$$\begin{array}{cccc} A & B & C & D \\ 1 & 2 & 3 & 4 \end{array}$$

And play Cross Harp on a **D** harmonica. It had always worked before.

Another approach was to play Straight Harp. If the song were in the key of **A** minor, he would count up 3 steps to figure out that **A** minor was the relative minor of the **C** chord. He would then play Straight Harp on a **C** harmonica.

A B C
1 2 3

If the song were in **D** minor, he'd count up 3 steps and play an **F** harmonica in the Straight Harp style.

D E F
1 2 3

But on "Volcano Mouth" neither Straight nor Cross Harp were worth beans. They didn't follow the tune. It sounded as though he were trying to wedge riffs into spots where they didn't belong. What was he going to do?

Now, with the rock facade of the theatre clearly in sight, Stone's mind started working with desperate energy. What he needed was a new harp style. All the styles he had learned so far were based on the locations of the Notes of Resolution.

For instance, playing Cross Harp, the Notes of Resolution were 2 draw, 3 blow, 6 blow, 9 blow, and, of course, the Cross Harp Draw Chord, holes 1234 drawn at the same time. Blowing Straight Harp, the Notes of Resolution were 1 blow, 4 blow, 7 blow, 10 blow and holes 1234 blown at the same time. Hmmm, he thought, Maybe... just maybe...

Stone placed his **G** harp to his puckered lips and played a 4 draw. Then he played 5 blow, 5 draw, and back to 4 draw. "That's it!" he said aloud. "That's it! USE 4 DRAW AS A NOTE OF RESOLUTION."

His heart beating to the joyous rhythm of making a new discovery, Stone walked around the back of the theatre and sat himself down near some garbage cans. For the next hour, the Cave Boy harmonicist sat there and learned as much as he could about this new harp style – the style he would call SLANT HARP.

172

The Slant Harp Approach

Slant Harp is a rock and blues style that gives riffs and solos a slightly different feeling than Cross or Straight Harp. It creates a sound that is partly bluesy, partly melodic. It creates a MINOR KEY FEELING.

The Slant Harp Formula is to play a harp in the key that is two steps down the scale from the key the guitarist is playing in. For instance, if the guitarist is playing in the key of **E** minor, count back two steps (including the **E**), and play a **D** harp.

$$A \quad B \quad C \quad \underset{2}{D} \quad \underset{1}{E} \quad F \quad G$$

And if the song is in the key of **A** minor, count back two steps from the **A**, and play a **G** harp.

$$D \quad E \quad F \quad \underset{2}{G} \quad \underset{1}{A} \quad B \quad C$$

This formula, of course, holds true for any minor key the guitarist chooses to play in.

Once playing the correct key of harmonica, all the Slant Harpist has to do is play riffs and patterns that use 1 draw, 4 draw and 8 draw as Notes of Resolution.

Slant Harp Notes of Resolution
1 Draw, 4 Draw, 8 Draw

The Slant Harp Wailing Notes are harmonizing notes that will not make a mistake at any point in the minor key variation of the I-IV-V chord progression.

Slant Harp Wailing Notes
5 Draw, 6 Draw, 9 Draw, 10 Draw

Usually, Stepping Stone Notes can be used as rungs on ladders between one harmonizing note and another. But playing Slant Harp, there are three Stepping Stone Notes that will clash with the music no matter how brief a time they are played. These notes to avoid are 2 draw, 3 blow and 3 draw.

The advanced Slant Harpist can bend 2 draw and 3 draw, and turn them into Wailing Notes. However, as mentioned earlier the beginner should stick to holes 4 draw and above. Because Slant Harp is played on the high end of the harp, it's good to start out on the lower-keyed harmonicas such as **G, A, B** or **C**.

The following page presents a Slant Harp Map showing where Wailing Notes, Notes of Resolution and Stepping Stone Notes are located.

Map of Slant Harp

10	Stepping Stone
(10)	WAILING
9	Stepping Stone
(9)	WAILING
8	Stepping Stone
(8)	RESOLUTION
7	Stepping Stone
(7)	Stepping Stone
(6)	WAILING
6	Stepping Stone
(5)	WAILING
5	Stepping Stone
(4)	RESOLUTION
4	Stepping Stone
(3)	Stepping Stone (avoid)
3	Stepping Stone (avoid)
(2)	Stepping Stone (avoid)
2	Stepping Stone
(1)	RESOLUTION
1	Stepping Stone

With the exception of 1 draw, all Slant Harp harmonizing notes are on 4 draw or above. For this reason, Slant Harp is usually played on the upper end of the harmonica – between 4 draw and 10 draw.

175

Slant Harp Riffs

As Stone sat near the garbage cans furiously trying to discover the secrets of Slant Harp, a group of children approached.

"Hey!" one of them cried, "It's Stone, the harp player."

The single voice soon turned into a chorus. "It's Stone. It's Stone!" Then the girls and boys crowded around the hurried harp player. "What's it like to play harmonica?" one of the boys asked. "What's it like to be a star?"

Stone glanced up at the little ragamuffins in their tattered sheepskin tunics and their dirty faces. "Well," he said, "It's, it's..." Finding no words to express the joy, the disappointment, the pressures and the privileges of being a star, Stone placed his **G** harp to his puckered lips. "It's like this..." he said.

As the children looked on, Stone played the Basic Slant Up Riff, the easy run he had decided to use as the basis for the harp work on "Volcano Mouth."

He started with the Note of Resolution, 4 draw, and slid the harp, without stopping his breath, to Wailing Note 5 draw. From here he played the 6 blow and wailed on the Wailing Note 6 draw.

"That sounds great!" the children cried. "Play some more!" To the sounds of clapping hands and shouts of "That's it, Stone, get down and boogie!" Stone played the Slant Down Riff.

Slant Down Riff
ⓖ 6 ⑤④

"Yeah!" the kids shouted, "Get it on, Stone!" As Stone continued exploring the possibilities of Slant Harp, a little boy, no longer able to contain himself, started dancing. The other children formed a circle and clapped their hands.

Here are some of the Slant Harp Riffs Stone played. They are presented in diagrams so that, hopefully, you will play them, too.

To start out, Stone played the Ultra Slant Up and Down Riff. This run used the same idea as the Basic Slant, but enhanced the minor key sound even more.

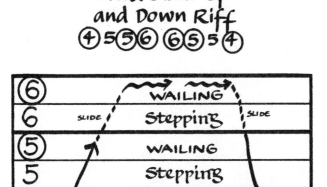

Then Stone moved up an octave and played the Basic Slant Riff on holes 8, 9 and 10.

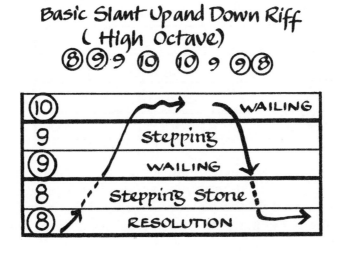

Now he switched to the Ultra Slant Up and Down Riff on holes 8, 9 and 10.

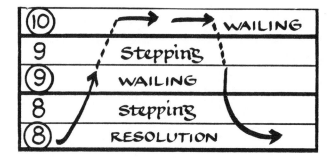

Amidst the handclapping, dancing and laughing, Stone decided to try an even more complex run. He would play a riff that went from Note of Resolution 4 draw up to Note of Resolution 8 draw.

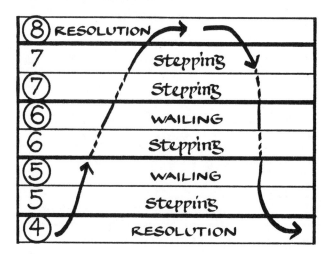

"That's great!" the kids shouted. "Play some more." Stone looked at his watch. The show would be starting soon. He felt pretty confident that Slant Harp would do the trick on "Volcano Mouth," and he knew it was time to get inside the studio. But he couldn't tear himself

178

away from the crowd of girls and boys who now were dancing with their hands in the air, their faces beaming.

"This is it," Stone thought. "This is why I wanted to be a good harmonica player. Not to become a star, not to become famous and make lots of money. No. I learned to play harp so I could bring joy and happiness into the world. So I could help people forget their problems. So I could make them feel good."

Inspired by this realization, Stone played the ultimate Slant Harp riff: the Slant Harp Scale.

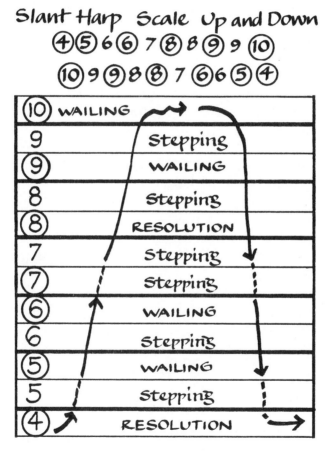

"Oh, wow!" the children shouted. "Wowwwwww!"

Now Stone wanted to really get down and play. Starting from the 4 draw, he played a long bending Note of Resolution, slipped to the 5 draw, the 6 blow, the 6 draw – wailing, warbling, tonguing, bending...

Then, the back door to the theatre suddenly opened, and the gruff face of the theatre manager appeared from the darkness. "Hey! You kids!" he shouted, "You get out of here or I'll call the police! You're making so much noise they can hear you inside." Then he spied Stone sitting beside the garbage cans. "And you, you old bum!" he spat at the greatest harp player who ever lived, "You get out of here, too. Shame on you for making these kids misbehave."

"But that's Stone!" a little girl shouted breathlessly. "That's the harp player for Umm and the Cave Boys."

The theatre manager moved closer. Catching a clearer glimpse of Stone's famous face, the theatre manager turned more colors than a smoggy sunset.

"Excuse me, Mr. Stone," he said, gruff voice now reduced to a whimpering falsetto. "I thought...I thought...oh well...you'd better come in right away. Everyone's looking for you. The show's about to start. Please, c'mon in. Please..."

Stone rose from his place behind the smelly cans. "And what about them?" he asked, pointing at the kids.

"What about them?" the manager asked.

"I want to play for them. I want to know I'm doing some good with all of this superstar hoopla."

"Well..." the theatre manager said. "I guess they can sit in the empty seats in the balcony."

"Whooppeeeee!" the children shouted.

The Show

The theatre's back stage was not as nice as the alley. The air was hot and stale, filled with the smells of sweat and makeup, B.O. and cologne.

"Right this way, Mr. Stone," said the theatre manager as he led the harp player past a line of scantily-dressed chorus girls. "Right this way."

Suddenly, Umm rushed up out of the darkness. "Stone!" she cried. She threw her arms around the harp man's neck. "Oh Stone, I was afraid you weren't going to show up. Listen, I don't care how your harp sounds. You're an important member of the Cave Boys. If you don't play, I don't sing."

Stone looked at her in surprise. "I thought nothing was more important to you than your career."

"You're just as important," Umm said. "And don't you forget it."

"You can say that again," added a familiar voice. It was Krok, holding his guitar. Behind him stood Gref and Smash.

"Hey," said Krok, "I'm sorry I got so uptight. This band wasn't any good 'til you joined it. You're playing harp with us – whether you want to or not."

"That's the way I feel too," said Gref.

"Me, too," added Smash.

"Okay," said the manager, "Enough of this emotion stuff. What's that have to do with rock and roll? You guys are ON!"

As the manager stepped to the side, the curtains rolled back and Stone suddenly realized that he was standing in front of 5,000 whistling, cheering people. As the cameras moved in, Dinah Sledgehammer was saying, "And now, the group you've been waiting for, Umm and the Cave Boys."

Krok approached the microphone. "We wanna play a new song for you. This is 'Volcano Mouth'."

The Cave Boy guitarist rose his hand in a wide arc and brought it down on the **A** minor chord. The bass and drums kicked in. The rhythm had a jungle pulse, a primeval beat that made the bones shiver. Wearing a black and gold tiger fur mini dress, Umm danced across the stage. Hair swirling through the air, she grabbed the microphone and started to sing.

"Volcano mouth, volcano mouth
Your mouth is exploding!
        exploding!
        exploding!
Yeahhhhhhhhhhhhhhhhh!"

The people in the audience looked at one another. What was this music? What did it mean? Some folks stood up and waved their arms. Others actually moved their hips, thighs, shoulders and hands to the infectious rhythm. Krok nodded at Stone and the harp man started to put what he had learned about Slant Harp into practice.

He wailed on 4 draw, slipped easily to 8 draw, back to 4 draw. He bent the 4 draw down, brought it back up, slid to 6 draw, blew on 7, sucked on 8, cascaded down to 4 draw in a minor key swirl of sound. His music was perfect for "Volcano Mouth."

Umm, Krok, Gref and Smash looked at Stone with relief and amazement. It was one thing to tell the Cave Boy harp player that he was more important to them than fame and success – quite another to believe it. But now they did believe it. Stone and his harmonica were incredible!

"Oh yeah!" the people in the audience shouted. This was the kind of music they'd always wanted to hear. Umm danced across the stage, whipping the mike cord behind her. Krok dipped to one knee and strummed his chords with robot-like precision. Gref and Smash grinned at one another and Stone wailed like a cave boy possessed.

What a show!

As the audience watched this spectacle of sound and movement, many found themselves thinking that Umm and the Cave Boys were like gods. Gods with the power to turn noise into music, silence into joy, boredom into excitement. And if not gods, then Umm and the Cave Boys were stars, stars as bright and beautiful as any in the heavens.

Few members of the audience realized they were watching the fruits of a long and often tedious labor, that Umm and the Cave Boys were like anyone else, that they fought and got angry with one another, that they were haunted by fears, frustrations, and deep, undefined yearnings for love and acceptance.

Fewer still realized that this vulnerability, this *humanity*, combined with a love for music, a capacity for joy and a need for self-expression, was the source of the magic that now filled the stage and seeped out into their lives. And almost no one was aware that the people themselves also were gods, goddesses, stars, heroes, heroines, what-have-you. No, the music was far too hot and the show too good for this kind of philosophizing.

Stone finished his solo to a standing ovation. Smash's drums rolled and thumped, stampeding the music into the second verse. The lyrics of the second verse were no more profound than those of the first. But who cared? All *anyone* heard was the pounding rhythm, the rich texture of Umm's voice, the razor-sharp slashes of Krok's guitar, the throbbing cry of Stone's harmonica.

Then, as quickly as the magic had begun, it stopped. The song was over. Band members hugged and shook hands. Applause washed over them like tumultuous waves of love.

"Umm and the Cave Boys!" Dinah Sledgehammer was shouting. "Umm and the Cave Boys!"

Krok grasped Stone's hand and looked him in the eye.

"Hey, man," he said, "that was the most incredible harp solo I ever heard you play."

The two musicians stood on the stage, the glow of their mutual success cutting through the rivalries, the arguments, the ego trips that had, for years, kept them from realizing how much they meant to each other.

"Tell me," Krok said. "How do you do it? How?"

"Talent," Stone said. "Sheer talent." Then the Cave Boy winked. "And a little help from my friends."

Notes

* SLANT HARP is a style of harmonica that sometimes sounds better than Cross Harp when accompanying songs in minor keys.

* The Slant Harp Formula is to count back two steps from the key the music is in. If the song is in the key of **B** minor COUNT BACK TWO STEPS (including the **B**) and play an **A** harp.

A   B   C   D   E   F   G
2   1

* When playing Slant Harp, the Notes of Resolution are 1 draw, 4 draw and 8 draw.

* Since Slant Harp is usually played on holes 4 draw and above, it works best on the lower-keyed harps such as **G** and **A**.

ELEVEN

Hubie's Blues or Everything I Almost Forgot to Put in the Book

So ends the saga of Stone, Umm, Krok, Gref and Smash. In Chapter XI, you and the author will meet an unforgettable character, learn some additional information on harp playing, and perhaps come to believe in a strange theory of musical reincarnation.

Hubie's Blues

Do you believe in reincarnation?

I didn't used to. Then I met Hubie. He was down at the bus station, sitting on his suitcase, softly playing the harmonica.

I couldn't hear him too well, so I moved closer. He was playing a Cross Harp style. I recognized some of the riffs. The tone was familiar, too. Still, there was something special about this guy's playing. It had those extra touches of feeling and grace that distinguish a good harpist from a pro.

He looked at me through his dark glasses and said, "Hey, You're Gindick, aincha?"

"Sure I am," I replied, flattered that a player this good would know who I am.

"Recognized you by your picture," he said. "Read your book, *The Natural Blues and Country Western Harmonica.*"

"What did you think?" I asked him.

"Good book for beginners. 'Course, no book is going to do it all. A guy or gal can know everything there is to know about the harp, and still not play it with any feeling."

"Unfortunately, you can't teach feeling," I said.

"Yeah, but you can encourage people to use feeling. Everybody's got it. It just comes out of some folks easier than others."

"Look," I said, "I'm writing a new book on harp playing. It's called *Rock n' Blues Harmonica.* I wonder if you'll take a look."

"Sure," he said.

188

I got into my suitcase and pulled out the tattered manuscript I'd been working on for months. "This is it," I announced, and handed it to him. I wondered if my new book had "feeling."

As he thumbed through the pages, I summarized the book for him. "It starts out telling people about the structure of music. Then it moves into the harmonica, explaining Straight Harp, Cross Harp and Slant Harp. Then it shows a bunch of riffs, how to play riffs in the I-IV-V progression, how to bend notes, how to use your hands . . ."

"Hmmmm," he said. "Looks pretty good, but I think you're leaving out some stuff people might want to know."

"Like what?" I asked, fighting the defensiveness that was creeping into my voice.

"Oh, stuff like using microphones and amps, the difference between using harp as a lead instrument and as a filler, tongue blocking, position playing, good harp players to listen to."

"Guess I could add another chapter," I muttered.

"Yeah, write another chapter and name it after me. Name's Hubie." He held out his hand and we shook.

"I can see it now," he chuckled. "Everything I Forgot to Put in the Book, or Hubie's Blues."

"Great title," I agreed.

"BUS 827 LEAVING IN 20 MINUTES FOR BAKERSFIELD," boomed a voice over the loud speaker.

Hubie looked at his watch. "Don't have much time," he said.

"Well, tell me what to write," I said, pulling out a pen and pad.

"Okay," Hubie said, "Let's start with microphones."

Sitting there on his suitcase, Hubie began explaining microphones to me. I wrote as fast as I could, and had some difficulty reading my writing later. Nonetheless, I think I got the gist of it.

189

The Art of Electric Harp

"I like to play country blues, folk blues, country western blues harp," Hubie said, "and in most cases, I play these styles by playing into a vocal mic sitting in a mic stand. But I also love rock and blues, and let's face it, most blues and rock harmonica is *electric* harmonica. Blowing your blues into a raspy-voiced, hand-held mic plugged into a pair of pounding 10" speakers, blasting it out like an electric guitar or sax onto some crowded, beer-smellin' dance floor while the band cooks . . . heck . . . that's about as good as it gets."

"Make this a rule: Every person who wants to play electric harmonica has to get the CD, *The Best of Muddy Waters*. The granddaddy of electric harp, Little Walter Jacobs, plays on every cut. Little Walter played in the 40's and 50's, and he pretty much set the standard for every blues player who has followed. Get his music into your bones by listening. Listen to Little Walter's tone and the way he plays the riffs. *Listen* to the nuances. *Study* this music with your ears. Why? Because that's your education. Little Walter 101.

"Now, say you're coming along. You've bought a few other keys of harps and you'd like to get that big electric sound. Well, you're gonna have to get yourself a mic and an amp, and learn a few techniques. See, the start of real rock n' blues harp is the handheld microphone. You cup the mic right into the harp and you play in the handcupped position.

"There are two basic kind of mics that harp players use. The first is the DYNAMIC, which pretty accurately reproduces the sounds that come into it. A lot of great harp players—from Paul Butterfield to James Cotton to John Popper—have used dynamic mics. They're built to pick up the sounds of a variety of musical instruments—

everything from violin to guitar to trombone to the human voice singing. You can tell which harp player is using the dynamic because these mics are usually ball-ended.

"The second type is shaped more like a bullet. It's called a CRYSTAL or BULLET mic. This is an old fashioned mic originally used in broadcasting in the 30's and 40's. These mics (which break if you drop them) were designed to cut through static, crowd noise etc. Frankly, they have pretty lousy fidelity. But, as the great blues players from the 40's and 50's discovered, they make a well-played blues harp sound great. These days crystal mics are made expressly for harp players. The best ones—and most difficult to use—are the Astatic, the Green Bullet, the BluesBlaster.

"But there are also guys who are inventing new mics, like Shaky Joe Harless out of Arizona. This cat makes the SHAKER—a smaller, easier-to-use mic with a built-in volume control and a sound as deep and rich as Southern molasses.

"You can also scour garage sales for a truly old mic, and maybe buy it for a song. You can get some really wicked old stuff. That $5 dictaphone mic you bought from your next door neighbor might be the best blues mic yet (or worst). Get adapters from Radio Shack and you'll be able to make all the connections.

"Now, you can plug your mic, be it old, new, crystal or dynamic, into lots of weird places. Most harp players agree electric harp sounds best played through a tube amplifier. Hard core blues guys get the FENDER TWIN REVERB BASSMAN or another tube driven amp of the same ilk. These antique guitar amps are what harp players used in the '50's. They get incredible deep, rich, warm sound with the handheld mic. Problem is: you have to turn these behemoth tube amps up really loud to get their benefits.

"Beginners will do fine with a smaller, less expensive PRACTICE AMP (usually solid state). Important features are 'GAIN' and 'VOL-UME' so you can get distortion, 'REVERBERATION' for a echo, and a line-out so you can plug your amp into the P.A. when performing with a band. You can get real portable with the battery-operated PIGNOSE AMP. Or, get your yourself a ROCKMAN, which is the size of a Walkman radio and plays through headphones.

191

Getting Great Amplified Tone

"So let's assume you have an amplifier and a mic. To get started, try to form a airtight cup with your hands that includes the mic and the harp. Bring this gourd of flesh and metal to your face, and lay the sides of your thumbs on your cheekbones to make a complete enclosure. That's how you hold the mic and harp.

"About plugging in . . . first, turn the volume all the way down! As you softly play a 2 draw or 6 blow, slowly turn the volume up until you can hear yourself through the speaker.

"Now let's set the levels of the bass, treble, gain and volume. As a prelude to what I'm going to say: rule of thumb, for harmonica, emphasize the bass and midrange. Turn the high frequency or treble sounds down. The idea is to get as much "body" as you possibly can. Go for the meat of the note, that sweet spot that makes it so rich.

"Almost all amps have separate 'gain' and 'volume' controls. The higher you turn the 'gain' up and the 'volume' down, the more distortion is produced. DISTORTION (with a hint of reverb) is the essence of that electric sound. It's gritty and modern and makes the harp as powerful as any other instrument on the stage. Think of it as the gonads of electric harp (can you say that in a harp book?) At first, everyone uses as much distortion as they can get, but eventually they back off into a clearer more pleasing, slightly distorted tone.

"Now let's talk REVERBERATION and the part it plays in great electric harp. Reverberation gives the harp an echo—and what could be better than that? So use it! Problem is: if you use too much reverb, your harp tone gets tinny and nonsubstantial." He tapped his ear. "You have to listen. *Really* listen and experiment. The main rule is this: never use so much effect that what your listeners hear is the effect, rather than the harp.

"I also think your readers should know about special effects such as DIGITAL DELAY—which produces incredible echo effects on demand and OVERDRIVE—which allows you amazing distortion

192

Two Sample Level Settings for Harp Players

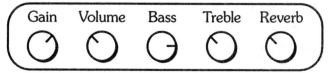

Typical raunch blues tone. High distortion at medium volume.

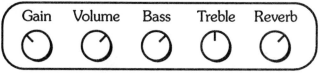

Prettier, softer tone with less distortion and more reverb.

without have to tweak your amp. These electronic boxes are staples for electric guitar players and can be equally important in good electric harp. If you're in search of greater variety in your sound, these may be the answer, especially if your amp isn't the best.

"Now that the levels are set, back away from the amplifier (maybe turn it up a little bit first!) and assume that fully handcupped position with harp and mic. Getting feedback or warnings of it? Get rid of it by doing any of these things:

    1. Move mic away from speaker's direction.
    2. Turn treble or higher frequencies down.
    3. Turn down the volume.

"Concentrate, and play a long, well-puckered 3 blow or 2 draw. If your hands form an airtight seal between mic and harp, and if your volume's sufficient,that note no longer sounds like a harmonica. Instead, it's more horn-like, or sounds like a fuzzed-out electric guitar. Try it on a wailing 4 draw. Bend that note down and bring it up. Don't be afraid of your sound, rather, milk it! Remember: GRITTY IS GOOD.

Hubie got up off his suitcase, and looked down the road. "Think that bus is late." Suddenly a harp appeared in his hand and he began to play a lonesome waiting-for-the-bus blues.

Tongue-Blocking for Octaves, Sophisticated Chords and That Deep Blues Pulse

This guy was good. Along with his riveting single notes, he kept coming back to this one technique — a sound like a bluesy accordian, separate notes warbling at the same time. It was uncanny. I finally stopped him. "What are you doing?"

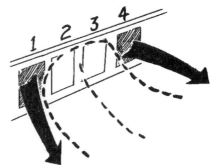

"Tongue-blocking octaves," said Hubie. "Draw 1234, and use your tongue to cover holes 23. The result is 1 and 4 draw playing at the same time: octaves. On your **C** harp, it's a funky **D** chord. This the old-fashioned way of playing harp, but it's coming back into style— especially among amplified blues players.

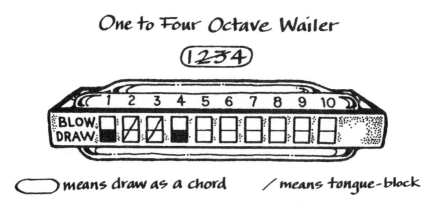

One to Four Octave Wailer

(1234)

⟨⟩ means draw as a chord   / means tongue-block

"Because it plays out Wailing Notes 1 and 4 at the same time, the 1 to 4 Octave Wailer is exactly that. It expresses the V chord. It creates tension . . . and is a very interesting sound. Subtle changes in the placement of your tongue easily change this sound. For instance, as soon as I lift my tongue so 23 draw are also playing, I've got the Cross Harp Chord of Resolution, 1234 draw.

194

Cross Harp Chord of Resolution
(1234)

"One approach to accompanying the deep Muddy Waters blues is setting up a tension by playing the 1234 draw chord and lifting the tongue on and off the harmonica or, just as good, wiggling it back and forth across the stops.. And you know all that stuff about the sensual harmonica? Don't forget about the tongue! The idea is to set a pulse, using a good strong stomach tremble.

(1234)	(1234)	(1234)	(1234)
tongue	no tongue	tongue	no tongue

"Slide up a hole and you're tongue-blocking 2 draw and 5 draw, another way to express resolution.

Two to Five Octave Resolution
(2345)

"Play Wailing Octaves at 3 draw and 6 draw, by tongue-bocking 4 and 5 draw, and even letting a little of the 2 draw in.

(3456)

"Or, play your blow Notes of Resolution 3 blow to 6 blow, by tongue-blocking holes 45 blow.

3456

"Explore the entire tongue-blocking range going up and down your harp. Really relax your tongue, sometimes moving it as though you were licking the holes of your harp. This is great for both acoustic and electric harp. Over time, you'll start incoporating the ol' tongue-block into more and more of your music. Sometimes you'll pucker, and sometimes you'll tongue-block."

And Don't Forget the Headshake!

Wailing on the 4 draw, Hubie started moving his harp back and forth across his lips. The result was a startling two-note cavalcade of hipness that made the hairs on the back of my neck stand at attention and dance.

"That's the headshake," Hubie said, "All you have to is slide the harp (or move your lips) between 4 and 5 draw very quickly as you get a single note. It's like using the same airstream on two different notes. It's relatively easy and it sure sounds good—especially when you bend the note down and bring it back up.

"You can do the headshake all over harp, but playing Cross Harp diatonic, some of the best ideas are 4 and 5 draw, 2 and 3 draw, and 3 and 4 draw, and 5 and 6 blow.

←→ means headshake

"In addition to bending, you can headshake as you get tongue-blocked-octaves and chromatic harp harmonies. Amplify this with lots of reverb and you've got another Little Walter specialty.

"When I say 'move the harp back and forth,' I don't mean to limit you. Some guys move it up and down very quickly, others side to side, others slant it. The point is the single note headshake is one of the easiest of all the techniques I'm describing. It's also versatile—working for blues, rock and country. It's an easy way to sound as though you've been playing for years, even when you've only been playing for days, and will get any audience applauding almost immediately. So tell your readers to use it!"

<u>D</u> Blues on the <u>C</u> Chromatic

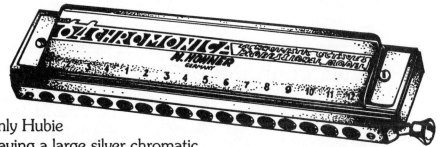

Suddenly Hubie
was playing a large silver chromatic
harmonica, and man, did it sound good.

I had fooled around with a chromatic, had learned a few songs, but
when it came to jamming I always got lost with the slide, not knowing when to press it in or let it out. I also couldn't bend notes on the
crazy thing—which has always seemed like a prerequisite for the
blues.

But now, Hubie was making his chromatic sound bluesy, even jazzy,
with big tone, big chords, no bends—that Little Walter sound. I
pulled my '64 Chro' from my harp bag. It felt big and intimidating in
my hand as Hubie quit playing and started to teach.

"Now the chro' is usually overlooked by people who already play the
10 holed diatonic because it's biggger, and because they can't figure
out the slide." Hubie shook his head. "This is a real shame because
the chromatic harmonica is a monster, and, as a lot of great
bluesmen prove, all you have to do with the slide is: IGNORE IT.
That's right, stop fiddlin' around with the damned thing. Now the
instrument is a lot simpler."

This made me laugh. I always thought I'd have to *master* the slide.
Instead, to play the blues, I had to *forget* about it.

"What we do is play this instrument 3rd Position Slant Harp style,
emphasizing the draw chords and the draw notes. By
emphasing the draw notes you get an automatic blues/jazz scale in
the key of **D.** Or, you can press the slide in, and keep it in, and
play in the key of **E** flat. Either way, Notes of Resolution are 1 draw
(both bass and midrange), 5 draw and 9 draw. And, avoid 4 draw
like the plague, because it's a Clash Note!

"On the chro' 64 (my favorite), the first four holes are bass notes. These are exactly the same as holes 5 through 8, only an octave lower. Skip over them for now and go to the fifth hole where the numbers start again and go up to 12.

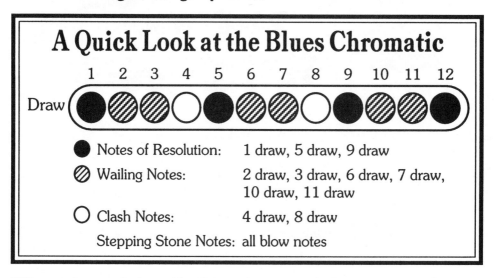

"The midrange 1 draw (the D note) is a good place to start. The basic idea is to take draw/blow patterns up and down your harp, always skipping over 4 draw and 8 draw because they're not part of the scale resolving on 1 draw or 5 draw or 9 draw. Some chromatic riffs are . . ." And he began to play a sweet chromatic harp blues.

Midrange Chro' Blues Scale
① 2 ② 3 ③ 4 ⑤
⑤ 4 ③ 3 ② 2 ①

Upper Range Chro' Blues Scale
⑤ 6 ⑥ 7 ⑦ 8 ⑨
⑨ 9 ⑦ 7 ⑥ ⑤

The Up Riff
①②3   ⑤⑥7⑦

The Down Riff
③3②①   ⑦7⑥⑤

198

Position Theory: Playing C Harp in Seven Different Keys

Hubie had his harps out and was on a roll. "I want to talk to you about another thing entirely, position playing. See, you've got First Position Straight Harp, Second Position Cross Harp, Third Position Slant Harp. I'm going to show you Fourth, Fifth, Sixth, and Twelfth Positions."

"Tell me what you mean by a position." I said.

Hubie thought for a moment before answering. "Although **C** harp was originally made to be played in the key of **C**, by choosing a different note for your Note of Resolution, you can play in different keys. Because the harp has missing notes, you get different scales, modes and musical feelings." With his toe in the dust floor, Hubie drew a circle, and put a little notch at 12 o' clock. "This chart helps me remember how this goes."

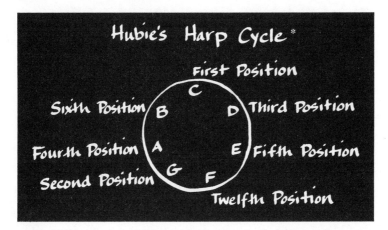

"When I play a **C** harp and resolve my a riff on a **C** note, using either 1 blow, 4 blow, 7 blow and 10 blow for my Notes of Resolution, I'm playing **First Position Straight Harp.** It's **C** harp in the key of **C** and where the Circle starts.

---

* This chart is an abridgement of The Circle of Fifths.

First Position Straight Harp Up and Down

1 2 ③
1 2 ③③ 2 1   (C Harp, Key of C)

"Count five steps on the circle and resolve that **C** harp in the key of **G**, using 2 draw, 3 blow and 6 blow and 9 blow— **G** notes—for Notes of Resolution,. This is **Second Position Cross Harp, C** harp played in **G**.

Second Position Cross Harp Up and Down

3 ③ 4 ④
④ 4 ③ 3   (C Harp, Key of G)

"For **Third Position Slant Harp**, count up five more steps and resolve on the **C** harp's **D** notes, 4 draw, 1 draw, and 8 draw. Using these as Notes of Resolution, fashion a scale that lets you play **C** harp in the key of **D**. It'll be a minor key scale, usually somewhat bluesy of jazzy.

Third Position Slant Up and Down

④ ⑤ 6 ⑥
⑥ 6 ⑤④   (C Harp, Key of D minor)

"These are three completely different modes you can explore on one little harp. In fact, each scale has its own musical tradition, and even it's own Greek name.

"Now, if you count five steps up the Key Cycle from the **D,** you come to the key of **A,** and that's **Fourth Position,** playing your **C** harp in the key of **A**, or usually **A minor.** Notes of Resolution (**A** notes on your **C** harp) are 3 draw bent, 6 draw and 9 draw. The kinds of riffs you get are minor key, with a gypsy feeling. That's why I call it **Gypsy Harp**. Remember, to play **Fourth Position** on your **C** harp, you want your guitarist to be playing in the key of **A minor.**" Giving me that Cheshire grin, he proceeded to demonstrate.

200

Fourth Position Gypsy Up and Down

(3)↓ (3) 4 5   5 (4) (3) (3)↘   (C Harp, Key of A minor)

Fourth Position Gypsy Scale Up

(3)↓ (3) 4 (4) 5 6 (6)

Fourth Position Gypsy Scale Down

(6) 6 5 (4) 4 (3) (3)↘

High Gypsy Scale Up

(6) (7) 7 (8) 8 9 (10)

High Gypsy Down

(10) 9 8 (8) 7 (7) (6)

Fourth Position Gypsy Blues Cycle

V chord	(3)↓ (3) 4 5
I chord	5 (4) (3) (3)↘
IV chord	(3)↓ (3) 4 (4)
I chord	(4) 4 (3) (3)↘

6 Draw wailing resolver

(6) 6 5 (6)

Pretty soon I was getting into the act, bending and unbending that 3 draw just right to get a minor key feeling. This was fun and it was new. Hubie looked at his watch "Let's go on to **Fifth Position,**" he said. "Count up five steps from the **A,** and you come to the key of **E.** The **E** notes on your **C** harp are at 2 blow, 5 blow and 8 blow. These are the Notes of Resolution. The music you get here is a minor key jazz blues, reminiscent of Tom Waits or Ray Charles. The old boy who taught it to me called it Short Harp. To use your **C** harp in **Fifth Position,** get your guitar player going in **E minor.** Check it out." And he began to play.

Fifth Position Short Harp Up Riff

2 3 ③   (C Harp, Key of E minor)

Fifth Position Short Harp Down Riff

③ ③ 3 2

Short Harp Scale Up and Down (midrange)

2 3 ③④ 5
5 ④③③ 3 2

Short Harp Two to Eight Blow

(Up) 2 3 ③④ 5 6 ⑥⑦ 8
(Down) 8 ⑧⑦⑥ 6 5 ④③ 3 2

Middle Eastern Scale

2 ② ② ③③ ④ 5

"To find **Sixth Position,** count up five more steps from the **E** and play in the key of **B,** or **B minor.** Notes of Resolution are 3 draw unbent and 7 draw. To me, this is like big band blues." Hubie gave me a wide-eyed look and started playing. Out came a totally new harmonica sound, a wild hornblast from the trumpet of Harry James.

Sixth Position Jazzy Up and Down

③ ④ 5 ⑤　⑤ 5 ④③　(C Harp, Key of B minor)

"It's that 5 draw Wailing Note that gives it such a big band feeling," he said. "I love whipping out my **C** harp when a guy is playing in the key of **B minor** or **B minor 7th.** Dig it."

Sixth Position Jazz Scale

③ ④ 5 ⑤⑥⑦

Sixth Position High

⑦⑧ 8 ⑨ 8 ⑧⑦

Three and Four Draw Jam

③ ④③

"The last one I wanna show you is **Twelfth Position,**" Hubie said.

"What about Seven through Eleven?" I asked.

"Well," Hubie said, "those might be more theoretical than actual because they have to be played almost entirely on bent notes (though there are guys who do it). **Seventh Position** is in **F sharp,** which is 2 draw middle bend. **Eighth Position** is in **D flat** out of 1 draw bend. **Tenth Position** is in **E flat,** which is 2 blow bent, 5 blow bent and 8 blow bent (the easiest of the three). **Eleventh Position** is in **B flat,** middle bend in the 3 draw. Most guys just play a key of harp in a flat or sharp key, say **F sharp** or **E flat** in order to get these keys.

"But **Twelfth Position,** well, that's when you play your **C** harp in the key of **F** out of 5 draw and 2 draw bent. What you come up with is kind of a bluesy way to play a melodic scale. Try this:

Melody Twelfth Position Up and Down
⑤ 6 ⑥ 7   7 ⑥ 6 ⑤

The Almost Diatonic 12ᵗʰ Position Scale
⑤ 6 ⑥⑦ 7 ⑧ 8 ⑨

Twelfth Position Coltrane Up and Down
⑤ 6 ⑥⑦   ⑦⑥ 6 ⑤

204

"So how's this work in practical terms?" I asked.

"First, get familiar with riffs in all seven position. Then do what I do: carry a box of harps to your jams, always the big six, **A, C, D, F** and **G,** and a couple of flatted keys and a key chart. Tell you the truth, usually I play Second Position Cross Harp, but if the song is a smokey jazz in a minor key, I may want to try Third, Fourth, Fifth Positions. If it's a more ethnic sounding jazz, I'll try out Fourth Position. If it's a major key rock or blues rocker, I'll think about Second Position, Twelfth Position and First Position. If it's a melody, slow, folkish and major key, I'll work with First and Second. In the beginning, every tune is an experiment. And since I never know until I try, I find myself switching harps a lot until my curiosity is satisfied. Then, I start fashioning out my solo. This adds a lot of depth to my harp playing. Makes it more fun."

This, I could believe, for Hubie looked to me like a happy man.

Bring This Chart to Jams

To Play in Key of	Use These Harps for These Positions						
	1st	2nd	3rd	4th	5th	6th	12th
C	C	F	B♭	E	A♭	D	G
D	D	G	C	F	B♭	E♭	A
E	E	A	D	G	C	F	B
F	F	B♭	E♭	A♭	D♭	F#	C
G	G	C	F	B♭	E♭	A♭	D
A	A	D	G	C	F	B♭	E
B	B	E	A	D♭	G	C	F#
Notes of Reso-lution	1 blow 4 blow 7 blow 10 blow	2 blow 3 blow 6 blow 9 blow	1 draw 4 draw 8 draw	3 draw bent 6 draw 9 draw	2 blow 5 blow 8 blow	3 draw 7 draw 10 draw	2 draw bent 5 draw 9 draw
			Work best when music is in a minor key				

205

Playing the Diatonic Harp as a Chromatic Instrument

"If you can hear it in your mind, you can do it on the harp," Hubie suddenly said. "Potentially, you can play your little diatonic harp in all twelve keys. You'd bend your way into a chromatic scale instead of the eight toned scale that the diatonic harp was made for, and then play riffs or scales that resolve out of each of these twelve tones."

"Sounds impossible," I muttered.

"Thing is, you have to think chromatically for this to happen and keep exploring that harp past the limitations. Getting to be a harp player is an inner thing, and guys with chromatic minds have turned the harp into a chromatic instrument.

"Some guys get a chromatic scale out of a diatonic harp by putting windsavers over the reeds. These little pieces of plastic make bending a lot easier, though some people say they change the tone.

"Other guys use a technique called the overblow. The 5 blow overblow gives you a tone halfway between 5 draw and 6 blow, and the 6 blow overblow gives you tone between the 6 draw and the 7 blow. This was made famous by a guy out of Chicago called Howard Levy, a jazz pianist who decided he wanted play chromatic jazz on the diatonic harp. He discovered a way of bending those blow notes *up* and revolutionized the way advanced harp players think about their instruments.

"Nowadays, Second Position is a jumping off place for learning to play fluently in as many different positions as possible, and finally, being able to play the diatonic harmonica as though it were a chromatic instrument that has all 12 tones, sharps and flats. When you reach that point you're no longer playing positions, you're playing chromatic harmonica on a diatonic instrument." His eyes took on that special Hubie gleam, "Now that's a worthy goal is my estimation."

206

"On the other hand, what's important here is making music, not the number of positions you can play, or the number of bends you can achieve. As a guy I know said, 'If you can play three and a half positions, you're good.'"

"Sure, sure," I said. "Show me this overblow."

Overblowing, Overdrawing— Over the Top

Hubie pulled out a Golden Melody harmonica and quickly unscrewed the top plate. "Listen," he said and blew into hole five as he crimped the reed with his finger. The note swung upward and Hubie was suddenly playing a much higher note. "That's it," he said, "That's the overblow, a step and a half higher than the five.

"The trick is to get the reed next door to the one you're playing going in the opposite direction. Overblowing 5 blow, I slightly block-off the air going into the hole in such a way that . . . get this . . . the 5 draw starts playing a half step up."

"Come on," I protested.

"No, that's exactly what happens." He handed the reed plate to me. I used my fingernail to touch the top reed near its base, and, sure enough, as I blew, that note squealed upward with a tone not unlike one of those confetti-dangling, party horns.

"Whoa!"

"The idea now, " Hubie said, "is to figure out a way to get this effect without touching the reed with your finger. Some guys accomplish it by bending 6 draw as far down as they can and then blowing, keeping the mouth in the same position. A successful result is the 6 blow overblow, a **B flat** on your **C** harp, same note as 3 draw middle bend, but up an octave."

"Other guys describe that overblow motion as being a little bit like coughing on a blow bend.

"Another technique is you open up your harp, and carefully measure and close the gap on the reeds. This takes lots of experimentation and the proper tools, but man, when you're closing in on an overblow, a little open harp surgery can be just what the doctor ordered. Let me give you an idea of how a complete chromatic scale goes."

The Chromatic Scale on a Diatonic "C" Harp

C	Db	D	Eb	E	F	F#	G	Ab	A	Bb	B
1	①↓	①	1o	2	②↓↓	②	②	③↓↓↓	③↓↓	③↓	③

C	Db	D	Eb	E	F	F#	G	Ab	A	Bb	B
4	④↓	④	4o	5	⑤	5o	6	⑥	⑥	6o	⑦

C	Db	D	Eb	E	F	F#	G	Ab	A	Bb	B	C	Db
7	⑦o	⑧	8↓	8	⑨	9↓	9	⑨o	⑩	10↓↓	10↓	10	10o

↓ means bend   ↓↓ double bend   ↓↓↓ triple bend
o means overblow or overdraw
O means draw

I was trying my overblow on the 6 blow and it just wasn't coming. "Don't *try* to overblow," he said. "Try to stop the normal flow of air so the overblow can happen. You need a blocked feeling—and you use your mouth, throat, tongue and air pressure to get it. That blocked feeling is what make the opposite reed vibrate."

I kept trying it with small result— only a series of blurps, wholps, screeches and blats from this instrument I thought (before today) I had mastered. Finally, Hubie took pity on me. "Don't get too frustrated. This is a project that'll take a guy years." He looked at his harp happily. "It's nice to have something to look forward to."

Hubie's Guide to Improvising

Hubie looked at his watch and gave a laugh. "Man, you're lucky that bus is late."

I wasn't so sure. My head was spinning with all the new information and his voice was beating a drumtrack into my brain. But Hubie had drunk a cup of coffee and had eaten a candy bar. Now he was waxing poetic.

"Lemme see if I can put this all together," he was saying. "See, the anatomy of almost all art—be it painting, poetry, music or literature—is this: Create a pattern. Repeat the pattern. Now vary the pattern or complicate it. Then return to it. That's it, it's so simple, and yet so many people don't understand this when they start playing harp. They think they have to go all over the instrument, making each note different and fabulous, and what they end up doing is wandering aimlessly.

"Say you're learning Cross Harp, you can build your harp jam by repeating a pattern—for instance the Good Morning Riff—over and over to a solid strong and riveting beat. Get into your phrasing, using silence and sound to make that Good Morning Riff talk. Then change it. Say, wail on a 3 draw bent for 4 or 8 beats, up to 6 blow, play 6 Blow Down . . . whatever . . . then return to the Good Morning Riff and repeat it over and over. That's a song. Or a great solo. Simplicity and repitition."

"Come on, it's more difficult than that," I said.

"You can play things more difficult than that," he agreed, "and you will. But no matter how technically incredible a harp player may be, if he doesn't follow this basic format, his harp will be much fury all over the place, signifying nothing. The answer is this, man: Create a motif. Repeat the motif. Change it. Maybe change it again. Return to the motif. Do it all again. How you do it is up to you, but that's the key that opens the door to the Land of Harmonica Excellence. Hell, *Artistic* Excellence.

"Now let's talk about volume when playing amplified. You've gotta be loud, you gotta to stand out in order to play a solo that really has impact. But if you play too loudly, you get feedback. One trick is to put your amp to the side instead of directly behind you. Another is to put your amp on a chair and get the sound up to where your ears are. Most important, be aware.

"Then there's the whole question of when to play and when not to. Face it, if you play too much, other musicians will get resentful. So don't play every song, and don't play continuously through every song. Instead, try to get a grasp of the difference between fills and leads. The fill is playing a riff (or note) in between the phrases of singing. For example:

Singer: "My baby left me this morning!"
Harp fill: *"Wa wa"*
Singer: "I've been crying all day long."
Harp fill: *"Wa wa wa"*

"The biggest problem beginners have with this is they put too many notes into their fills. Keep it simple: many times all it has to be is one note. A sound that answers the singer's voice, a bend or a warble. Also, get a sense of the chord progression the band is playing. Know where it builds, where it falls, and how it ends so you can mold your music to the overall scheme of things. This is one reason to sit and listen to the music you're accompanying before you start.

"Once the verse and chorus ends, and you've done so well on the fills, it may be time to take the lead. The singer stops singing, the lead guitar player stops playing and everyone looks expectantly at you. Best advice: once you're given the lead, *take it!* Be aggressive as you string riffs together. Go for it with all your soul as you use the principles of motif and repetition. This is *your* time, and people are watching you. They want to feel something, especially from you, the harp player. The thing is, your lead doesn't have to be difficult to perform. Beginners can start with a one note lead, say a 4 draw, artfully timed, imaginatively played. From here, build into more complex jams.

210

"When your lead is over, usually at the same point the chord progression has come back to the Chord of Resolution, back off for a verse, then go back to the fills that compliment the singer's voice instead of competing with it. Even if you're just a beginner, people love this kind of approach.

"Another approach to jamming with a band is to create a harmonica 'wall of sound.' For instance, play a perfectly tongue-blocked octave draw that you repeat over and over, building a tension, adding a chordal depth to the overall sound of the band. This is playing harmonica like an organ.

"Some harp players really identify with horns—trumpets and trombones, etc. They use phrases and tonal qualities that emulate the brassy style and precise timing of a jazz horn section. To me, Lee Oskar and Rod Piazza fall into this category. Other harp players emulate the fiddle, and there seems to be more swelling of their tone, resulting in a more passionate, human-voiced sound. Charlie McCoy and, in a different way, Sonny Boy Williamson II seem to have that approach.

"Others combine lots of different voicing styles into one unique approach. Say going from horn-style harp to fiddle to human voice—all in one phrase! One of the most interesting things about John Popper of Blues Traveller: he's the first harp player to emulate a synthesizer. One thing for sure, even though you should study the masters, strive to develop your own sound. Nobody sounds like Lee Oskar. Nobody sounds like Madcat Ruth. Nobody sounds like John Popper. Nobody sounds like Howard Levy. Amplified or unamplified, they each present different tones, techniques and styles.

"What else? Taste and sensitivity are more important than technical virtuosity and speed. Try to ascertain a melody and support it. The first rule is the same as your doctor's: do no harm. The second rule: don't be so cautious you might as well have not shown up.

"It's also important to talk about chord progressions that the guitar or piano plays. The main blues progression is I-IV-V, but that's just a jumping-off point. Just in the key of **G,** there are such beauties as **G–Em–C–D, G–Am–C–D** and the classic **G–F–C,** spinning off into an infinite variety of voicings, forms, sequences, timings and rythyms. Depending on your skill and on the melody, all of these forms will sound great played with Cross Harp or the positions, and will take your harmonica music beyond the blues.

"Finally, I wanna talk to you about INTONATION—playing in tune. See, the harp ain't a piano: you don't press a button and get a precise tone. The harp is more like the human voice: a little sharp, a little flat. The slightest change in the shape of your lips or the air pressure changes the pitch and tone of the harp, especially among players who bend a lot of notes. If you assume the harp is always on pitch, you might be mistaken. You might be bending that note out of tune or not bending when you need to. Maybe you're playing *all* your notes in a flattened position. Maybe none. The way you bring a bend up (or down) is just as important as the bend itself. You need to listen and pay attention to your intonation.

"One thing that will really help is to get the music inside of you. That's why you should study the music of the blues giants: starting with Little Walter and Big Walter, going to Sonny Boy Williamson II, Sonny Terry and Jimmy Reed.

"Fill yourself up with their music, and your music will come tumbling out. You should also listen to the great guitarists—and jam with them. I'm thinking of giants like Muddy Waters, John Lee Hooker, Stevie Ray Vaughn, Buddy Guy, B.B. King, Earl Hooker, Eric Clapton.

"There's a great blues scene happening right now. The music is both amplified and accoustic. You can hear it in clubs, on radio, at concerts. Blues festivals are great places to plug into the harmonica world, and most major cities have blues organizations. You'll hear great harp, meet other harp players, maybe even jam. Harp players are generally pretty good guys and the blues culture is filled with interesting intelligent people.

"And also learn something about the history of the blues and the blues harp: How it was forged out of the the lives and souls of black people in the south, an extension of African music of the 1600's, and lives on today as the most influential musical form of its day.

212

"Listen to the great harp players since World War II: George Smith, James Cotton, Paul Butterfield, Charlie Musslewhite, Junior Wells, James Harman, William Clarke, Sugar Blue, Magic Dick, Rod Piazza, Mark Wenner, Phil Wiggins, Mark Humel, Tom Ball . . . and so many more.

"Rock's premier players are Norton Buffalo, Stevie Wonder, John Popper and Howard Levy. But there are other guys, lots of 'em, who might be just as good. It's staggering—there are so many great players! People ask 'who's the best?' as though harp playing were a basketball game. The guy who's best is the guy who's blowing your mind at the moment. . . . and sometimes that's *you!*"

The Magic Harmonica

Suddenly a silver bus turned up the street and came noisily into the terminal. You could smell the exhaust and the grime of the road. Somehow, the harmonica fit this scene perfectly. People were scurrying around the bus station, lugging suitcases, saying their goodbyes.

Hubie gave me a grin. "Well, I gotta go . . ."

"Play something first," I said. "Just a lick. I'd like to hear you once more."

Hubie looked at the entrance to the bus. He pulled out his harp and cupped it in his hands. *Waaaaaaa!* the harp moaned. *Waaaaaah Taa Waa Wa!*

Lord, it was sweet!

"And that," he said, "is Hubie's blues."

213

He grabbed his suitcase and took a step toward the door. Then he stopped, turned around and shook my hand. He placed something hard and small in it. The next thing I knew he was climbing on the bus. From the sidewalk, I watched him make his way down the crowded aisle and sit next to a fetching blonde who seemed mighty glad to see him. Then three other guys appeared in the window and they all had a good laugh. Exhaust shot from the rear of the bus and they were off.

Goodbye, Hubie, I said to myself. Thanks for your help.

I was walking, looking for the snack bar when I realized that my hand was clenched around something Hubie had given me. It was a small, strange harmonica. I'd never seen anything like it.

I played a 3 blow, a 4 draw, a 6 draw and a 9 blow. I played the Up and Down Blues Riff, I played the Six Blow Down. I played a Good Morning Riff, I played the Good Morning Riff up to 3 draw, then 3 draw bent down. I couldn't stop playing!

Then I started bending. Low, throaty, growling bends. High soaring bends. Overblows, overdraws, playing positions, playing chromatic! The tone of this harmonica was incredible. It dripped like molasses, it soared like a rocket, it honked like a horn, it sang like a Streisand.

People were looking at me as my harp playing peaked on the bending 10 blow and tumbled through space, over the notes to the 2 draw. Some folks were smiling, tapping their feet. Others had disapproval on their faces.

Finally, I managed to wrestle the harmonica away from my lips. I looked at the harmonica more closely. Yes, this was it. This was the harmonica I'd been looking for all my life.

It was carefully carved from the tusk of a wild boar, and I felt sure that the reeds were from the hard bark of the boo boo tree.

214

Harp-Player's Resource & Music Index

The next few pages tell you what key you need to jam Cross Harp on each song with some wonderful CD's, records and tapes. How's it work? Put a CD in the player, find the right key harp for the song you want to play, and begin molding harmonica sounds to the sounds of recorded music. Start with your Wailing Notes. Create tension until the music demands resolution. Hey , you sound pretty good!

Cross Harp

Blues Brothers
Briefcase
Full of Blues
Harp: Dan Ackroyd

Can't Turn	F
Bartender	F
Messin'	E
Almost	A
Biscuit	B flat
Shot Gun	E flat
Groove Me	D
Don't Know	C
Soul Man	B flat
B Movie	A
Flip Flop	E flat
Turn You	F

Blues Traveler
Four
Harp: John Popper

Runaround	C
Stand	A flat/D
Look Around	C
Fallible	B
Mountains Win	C/D
Freedom	G
Crash Burn	D
Price to Pay	A
Hook	D
Good, Bad, Ugly	A/D/E
Just Wait	F
Brother John	A/C

Norton Buffalo
Lovin' in the
Valley of the Moon
Harp: Norton Buffalo

Lovin'	C
One Kiss	C
Ghetto	D flat
Nobody	A
Puerto	A
Hangin'	G
Another	B flat
Rosalie	B flat
Jig's Up	D
Eighteen	A
Sea	F

Jimmy Buffett
Changes in Latitudes
Harp: "Fingers" Taylor

Changes	G
Wonder	C
Banana	C
Tampico	D
Lovely	F
Margaritaville	G
Shelter	A
Miss You	F
Biloxi	D
Landfall	C

Paul Butterfield
East Meets West
Harp: Paul Butterfield

Walking Blues	D
Get Out	F
Gotta Mind	F
All These Blues	D
Work Blues	B flat
Mary Mary	D
Two Trains	B flat
Never Say No	B flat
East West	G

Ry Cooder
Bop 'Til You Drop

Sister	E flat
Go Home	A flat
Makes You Rich	F sharp
Work Out	A
Hollywood	F
Granny	D flat
Trouble	B flat
Mess Up	G
Win	B

James Cotton
High Compression
Harp: James Cotton

Potato	E
Yin	F
23 Hours	G*
Doggin'	C
Cuttin'	C
Doin' Bad	A
Sunny	D
Super Harp	F
EZ	C
Compression	C

*Although listing is for cross harp, James plays C chromatic in key of D.

Bob Dylan
Blonde on Blonde
Harp: Bob Dylan

Rainy Day	A
Pledging	D
Visions	D
Sooner or Later	B flat
Your Way	C
Achilles	C
Sweet Marie	G
I Want You	B flat
Memphis Blues	A
Pillbox Hat	D
Like a Woman	A
Fourth Time	A
5 Believers	D
Sad Eyed	G

Bob Dylan
Highway 61
Revisited
Harp: Bob Dylan

Rolling Stone	F
Tombstone	F
Train	D flat
Buick 6	F
Thin Man	G
Queen Jane	F
Highway 61	E flat
Tom Thumb	C
Desolation Row	A

Cross Harp

The J. Geils Band
 Best of the
 J. Geils Band
Harp: Magic Dick

Southside	C
Give It	C
Where Did	D
House Party	A
Detroit	F
Whammer	A
I Do	C
Must Got	F
Looking	F

Slim Harpo
 The Best of
 Slim Harpo
Harp: Slim Harpo

Mohair Slim	B
Keep What I Got	B
Scratch My Back	B flat
Buzz Me Baby	A
King Bee	B flat
Rainin'	C
Shake	D
Ten-ni-nee	D
Breadmaker	A
Tip On In	A

Walter Horton
 Big Walter Horton
Harp: Big Walter

Good Time	C
Christine	C
Lovin'	A
Boy Blue	B flat
Can't Hold	A
Sun	C
Tell Me	A
Mercy	G
That Ain't	A
Temptation	A
Trouble	D

Walter Jacobs
 Little Walter
Harp: Little Walter

My Babe	B flat
Hours	B flat
So Fine	A
Last Night	G
Blues Feel	G
Can't Hold	C
Back	B flat
Too Late	B flat
Feeling	D
Teenage	G
Fool	D
Saucer	G
Juke	A
Old World	B flat
Wall	C
Watch Yourself	A
Blue Lights	G*
Tell Mama	C
Gotta Go	D
Shade	A
Too Late	C
Thunderbird	G*
Baby	C
Boom	A

* *Walter played chromatic "C" harp in the key of D (1 and 4 draw notes of resolution) on these numbers. The "G" listing is for regular cross harp.*

Bob Marley
 Natty Dread

Lively Up	G
No Woman	F
Belly Full	F
Rebel	D
So Jah	G
Natty	D
Bend Down	F
Talkin'	D
Revolution	F

John Mayall
 Turning Point
Harp: John Mayall

Laws Change	F
Saw Mill	A
Gonna Fight	E
Hard Share	C
California	G
Roxanne	F
Room to Move	F sharp

Charlie McCoy
 The Real McCoy
Harp: Charlie McCoy

Today I Started	B
Orange Blossom	F
Only Daddy	A
Jackson	F
Hangin' On	A
Real McCoy	E
Lovin' Her	D
Easy Lovin'	E flat
How Can I	F
Help Me	A
Country Road	F

Willie Nelson
 Stardust
Harp: Mickey Raphael

Stardust	C
Georgia	F sharp
Blue Skies	F
All of Me	C
Unchained	C
September Song	D flat
Sunny Side	C
Moonlight	
Get Around	D
Someone	D

Lee Oskar
 Before the Rain
Harp: Lee Oskar

Rain	F sharp
Steppin'	D
SF Bay	F sharp
Feelin'	A flat
Words	F
Sing Song	F sharp
Haunted House	F

217

Cross Harp

Rod Piazza
Harpburn
Harp: Rod Piazza

Rockin' Robin	D
Bad Boy	C
California Boogie	A
Upsetter	A
Tribute	E*
Harpburn	G*
Feelin' Good	E flat
Honey Bee	F*
Cold Chill	A
Dangerous	G*

* Although the key listed is for cross harp, Rod plays chromatic on these numbers.

Bonnie Raitt
Sweet Forgiveness
Harp: Norton Buffalo

Leave Home	G
Runaway	F
Two Lives	B flat
Louise	D
Gamblin'	G
Forgive	E flat
Farewell	E flat
Three	E
Time	E
Home	A

Jimmy Reed
Upside Your Head
Harp: Jimmy Reed

Shame Shame	A
Baby	A
Ain't Got	A
Ain't Lovin'	B flat
Road	A
Bright Lights	D
Too Much	A
Big Boss Man	A
Upside	D
Good Lover	B flat
Honest	D
Virginia	D
Hush	C
Found Love	D
Baby What	A
Goin' NY	D

Madcat Ruth
Gone Solo
Harp: Madcat Ruth

Sweet Chicago	A
Changed	C
Bad Luck	E flat
Catfish	A
Fishin'	F
Shortnin'	F/G/A
Boom Jake	A
Too Late	C
St. James	F*
Help Me	D*
Hurts Me	C
Nobody	G*
Sonny Terry	D
Rollin'	D

*On St. James, Madcat plays F sharp in 5th position (2 blow note of resolution), In Help Me, he plays D harp in 3rd position (slant harp, 4 draw note of resolution). On Nobody, he plays G harp in 12th position (5 draw note of resolution).

George Smith
Oopin' Doopin' Doopin'
Harp: George Smith

Phone Blues	E
Blues in the Dark	A flat
Blues Away	E
Rockin'	E
California Blues	C
Oopin' Doopin'	G
Suzie Cross	D flat
Love Me	E
Down in N.O.	A flat
Found	D
Love	F
Ball	D

Bruce Springsteen
Darkness of the Edge of Town
Harp: Bruce Springsteen

Badlands	A
Adam	A
Something	C
Candy	F
Racing	B flat
Promised Land	C
Factory	F
Streets	D
Prove It	D
Darkness	C

Bruce Springsteen
Greetings from Asbury Park
Harp: Bruce Springsteen

Blinded	A
Growing Up	F
Arkansas	G
Bus Stop	C
Flood	C
Angel	C
For You	B flat
Spirit	A
Saint	D

Southside Johnny & the Asbury Jukes
The Time It's for Real

This Time	C
Without Love	B flat
Popeye	F
First Night	F
She's Got	D
Some Things	A
Little Girl	A
Fever	D
Love	C
Dance	C

Cross Harp

Bill Tarsha Rocket 88's
Let's Rumble
Harp: Bill Tarsha

Cookin'	D
Rumble	A
You Don't	G*
Walk In	E flat
Don't Know	B flat
Tongue	A
Breakout	D
Love	F
Elmo	A
Road	G*
That's All	E

We believe Bill plays a "C" chromatic in key of D. Listing is for regular cross harp.

Sonny Terry
Blind Sonny Terry
Harp: Sonny Terry

Cornbread	A
Ham	A
Lost John	A
Chain Gang Blues	A
It Takes a Chain	A
Betty Dupree	A
Stickhole	A
Rock Me	A
Chain Gang Special	G
Long John	A
Pick a Bale	A
Red River	A

Sonny Terry
Whoopin'
Harp: Sonny Terry

Eyes	B
Whoopin'	A
Burnt	C
Whoee	C
Crow	B
Tough	B
Whoee	C
Got Blues	A
Ya Ya	A
Roll Baby	B

Muddy Waters
Hard Again
Harp: James Cotton

Mannish Boy	D
Bus Driver	A
Wanna Be Loved	F*
Jealous	D
Satisfied	D
Blues Baby	D
Florida	C
Cross Cut	C
Little Girl	D

The listing is for Cross Harp, but James plays a "C" chromatic in the key of C on this number.

Muddy Waters
The Best of Muddy Waters
Harp: Little Walter

Just Make Love	G*
Long Distance	B flat
Louisiana Blues	D
Honey Bee	B flat
Rolling Stone	A
I'm Ready	A flat**
Hoochie Coochie	D
She Moves Me	B flat
I Want You	C
Standing	B flat
Still a Fool	B flat
Can't Be Satisfied	C

Little Walter plays chromatic Third Position. on the diatonic, play your G harp Cross Harp.
**Walter played C chromatic in pressed position D flat. Play Cross Harp diatonic on your A flat harp.*

Sonny Boy Williamson
Bummer Road
Harp: Rice Miller aka Sonny Boy Williamson II

Next to Me	B flat
Santa Claus	D
Little Village	F
Lonesome Road	F
Can't Do	D
Temperature	F
Unseen Eye	C
Hand Out	B flat
Open Road	E
This Old Life	E

Sonny Boy Williamson and the Yardbirds
Harp: Rice Miller aka Sonny Boy Williamson II

Bye Bye	C
Cool Blue	F
Stop	F
Eyesight	F
Memphis	D
Cross Heart	F
Crazy	C
9 below	F
Long Time	C
The Dead	F
Stop Baby	C
Down Child	C
Pontiac	F
Close	C

Neil Young
Hawks and Doves
Harp: Neil Young

Little Wing	E flat
Homestead	G
In Space	F
Kennedy	B flat
Staying	C
Coastline	F
Man	C
Coming	C
Jawks	C

Additional Resources for Harmonica Players

Kevin's Harps *(Kevin McGowan, editor)*
210 Farnsworth Ave., Bordentown, NJ 08505; (800) 274-2776

American Harmonica Newsletter *(Al Eichler, editor)*
2362 W. Territorial Road, Battle Creek, MI 48906

Harmonica Information Publication *(Winslow Yerxa, editor)*
203 14th Ave., San Francisco, CA 94118

Mississippi Saxophone *(Tim Moody, editor)*
3672 Game Farm Road, Springfield, OR 97477; (503) 726-5992

Easy Reeder
c/o Hohner, Inc., Post Office Box 15035, Richmond, VA 23227

Harmonica Happenings
Society for the Preservation of the Harmonica (SPAH),
Post Office Box 865, Troy, MI 48099
  (SPAH can tell you of a harmonica club in your vicinity.)

Harp-L *(Internet harmonica subscriber service)*
send e-mail to <majordomo@garply.com>
with message "subscribe Harp-L"

International Harmonica Organization *(Petter Janssen)*
Hollandhof 64, 5709 DB Helmond, Netherlands

Deutscher Harmonika Verband
Rudoplf-Maschke-Platz 6, 7218 Trossingen, Germany

National Harmonica League *(Colin Mort)*
Rivendell, High Street, Shiiel Heath,
Southhampton SO3 2JN, England

Mail order music companies for blues and country recordings are:

Roots and Rhythm
6921 Stockton Ave., El Cerrittos, CA 94530; (510) 525-1494

Elderly Instruments
1100 N. Washington, Lansing, MI 48099; (517) 372-7890

Alligator Records
Post Office Box 60234, Chicago, IL 60660; (800) 344-5609

Rock n' Blues Harmonica

cassette series by Jon Gindick

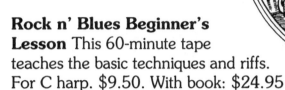

Learning to play harmonica
is much easier with cassette
lessons. Now you can hear
what you're trying to play.
Just stick that tape in the
player, pull out your harp and
start jamming.

**Rock n' Blues Beginner's
Lesson** This 60-minute tape
teaches the basic techniques and riffs.
For C harp. $9.50. With book: $24.95

Rock n' Blues Accompaniment Lesson is a *tour de force* of
instruction and playing for beginners and intermediates. 45 minutes.
For C, D, A, G harps. $9.50

Three Chords of the Blues is a jam-along lesson that teaches and
demonstrates every chord cycle in the book. 50 minutes. For C and
G harps. $9.50

Blues Harp, The Movie

Country and Blues Harmonica for the Absolute Beginner
An instructional video by B.B. King and Jon Gindick

Jon Gindick and blues guitar legend B.B. King made this superb
video to let you **hear** and **see** detailed instruction on how to play
the blues harp. You'll go over the basics—holding the harp, lip
shapes for single notes, how to bend notes, tonguing notes, using
your hands, bending and playing many of the riffs in this book to
guitar. Then you'll jam with B.B.—the man many call the most
influential blues guitarist of our time. 60 minutes of blues harp
instruction for $24.95.

Harmonica Americana

Learn to Play America's 30 Greatest Songs

Pucker up and play a haunting "Danny Boy," an incredible, blues-inspired "America the Beautiful," a side-splitting, lip-burning "Turkey in the Straw" and 27 other great songs. **Harmonica Americana** includes songs, lyrics, guitar chords, history of harmonica music, easy-play harmonica notation—plus a section on blues and train music. 176-page book $11.95

Harmonica Americana Cassette Lessons:

Volume I – "Basics"
Learn to play the great songs notated in **Harmonica Americana,** as Doc gives you slow-motion, step-by-step instruction on single notes, hands, tonguing, bending, playing the songs and more. Recorded in stereo for your C harp. A steal at $9.50.

Volume II – "Jam Along Songbook"
Here's Doc on his sweet-sounding ol' Martin guitar, playing his harp, and strummin' that big chord of C. He goes through the great songs, bringing them to life and letting you hear and play along with these American masterpieces. Larceny at $9.50.

Price Break!
Get both tapes for $18. Book included, $24.95.

The Jam Lessons

Harp and Guitar Jam Vol. 1
Jam with Jon to seven different guitar chord progressions. Includes country, jazz, rock, folk and blues styles.
G and C harps. 60 minutes $9.50

Harp and Guitar Jam Vo.l 2
Features blues, boogie, rock jams, and many tips on bending, and tongue-blocking and riff making.
For A harp. 60 minutes $9.50

The Four Positions of Blues, Rock and Jazz Harmonica.
Learn the secrets of 4th position (C harp in key of E), Straight Harp Blues (C harp in the key of C), Cross Harp melodies (C harp in key of G), 3rd position riffs and melodies (C harp in key of D minor). Includes easy guitar music for all four styles.
60 minutes $9.50

The Robert Johnson Lesson
Teaches you seven Robert Johnson blues classics. Includes "Rollin' and Tumblin,'" "Sweet Home Chicago," "Love in Vain" "Come in My Kitchen," " Dust My Broom," and "Walking Blues."
For C harp $9.50

Gospel Plow
This two-volume set teaches the Cross Harp way to play gospel standards "What a Friend We Have in Jesus," "Kum Ba Yah," "When the Saint's Come Marching In" and many others.
. . . .$14.95 for two tapes.

ORDERING INFORMATION
Cassettes are $9.50 for 1, $18 for 2, $26 for 3, $34 for 4, $41 for 5, $47 for 6, $54 for 7, $60 for 8, $65 for 9, $5 for each additional.

Send your check, money order or credit card info to:
Jon Gindick, 530 Ranch Road, Visalia, CA 93291
e-mail: JFGindick@aol.com

Add $3 shipping to all orders. California: add current sales tax.
Overseas: add enough shipping for airmail.

Special thanks to the guys and gals at Harp-L . . .
Mike Curtis, John Thaden
for their information, encouragement and support.

Thanks to Diane Mountford for
unwavering good cheer and excellent work.

And thanks, especially to
Linda, Georgia and Sylvia,
who add so much meaning.

ABOUT THE ILLUSTRATOR

Mark Zingarelli was born in Wilkensburg, Pennsylvania in 1952. Currently a leading force in San Diego's "artistic hotbed," his cartoons and illustrations are favorites in publications both national and international. He lives in San Diego with his wife, Linda.